One-Minute
PRAYERS™
for your
Adult Children

ALLISON BOTTKE

CW00951977

HARVEST HOUSE PUBLISHERS
EUGENE, OREGON

A list of Bible versions used is included in the back of this book.

Cover by Franke Design and Illustration, Minneapolis, Minnesota

Cover photo © Bertrand Demee / Photographer's Choice RF / Getty Images

Published in association with the Steve Laube Agency, LLC, 5025 N. Central Ave., #635, Phoenix, Arizona, 85012.

ONE-MINUTE PRAYERS is a series trademark of The Hawkins Children's LLC. Harvest House Publishers, Inc., is the exclusive licensee of the trademark ONE-MINUTE PRAYERS.

ONE-MINUTE PRAYERS™ FOR YOUR ADULT CHILDREN
Copyright © 2015 Allison Bottke
Published by Harvest House Publishers
Eugene, Oregon 97402
www.harvesthousepublishers.com

ISBN 978-0-7369-6243-8 (padded hardcover)
ISBN 978-0-7369-6244-5 (eBook)

Printed in China

14 15 16 17 18 19 20 21 / RDS-JH / 10 9 8 7 6 5 4 3 2 1

For Alicia

An adult child for whom many have prayed
and whom God has redeemed and restored for a great
and glorious purpose.
And for my Serenity Group.
I love you all.

A New Day Is Dawning

*Keep on asking, and you will receive what you ask
for. Keep on seeking, and you will find. Keep on
knocking, and the door will be opened to you. For
everyone who asks, receives. Everyone who seeks, finds.
And to everyone who knocks, the door will be opened.*

MATTHEW 7:7-8 NLT

Contents

Introduction

My Fellow Parent,

When our children officially become adults, the pendulum of legal responsibility might change, but the responsibility of the heart never does. We love them with every fiber of our being regardless of the choices they make. We ache for their security, and we long for them to find their purpose and appreciate their gifts and blessings. We desperately want them to feel the peace, joy, grace, and love of God.

Our assignment to pray for our adult children has no expiration date. Moms and dads everywhere continue to go to their knees in passionate prayer for their kids regardless of their age or the state of their relationship.

I love my adult son, and I have many joyful memories of our times together. However, I'm one of many parents who have struggled for years with how and when to apply tough love. I've tried to fix, rescue, and change my son—to no avail. I've watched him hit bottom and bounce more than a few times. I've talked, cried, and prayed with him through inch-thick security glass, prison bars, and salty tears. I have felt the bitter sting of guilt, shame, fear, anger, and despair as a parent. In these desperate places, I've grown closer to the God who loves me—and my adult child.

It doesn't take a village to reach God. It takes one heart willing to stop for one minute to pray. One heart that is open to say, "God, please give me direction and peace. Please hear the longing of my soul. And God, please be with my adult child and keep him (her) safe." We serve a God whose love, grace, goodness, and miraculous power are only a prayer away.

You may be blessed with a strong and healthy relationship with your adult child, or you might be in pain and quiet desperation. Either way, you can rest assured that God can and will show you His face and His love. We must believe unequivocally that God will hear and respond to our prayers for our children—in His time and according to His purpose.

But how can we ask God to give hope, peace, love, or direction to others when we ourselves are hopeless, restless, guilty, or lost? We can pray effectively for our adult children only when we pray effectively for ourselves. The two go hand in hand. Scripture teaches us that the prayer of a righteous man avails much.

We strengthen the bond of our relationships with our adult children when we come before God with prayerful, humble, repentant, teachable, and righteous hearts.

I invite you to join me in doing that now.

Allison

The Six Steps to Sanity

I introduced the Six Steps to SANITY in my book *Setting Boundaries with Your Adult Children: Six Steps to Hope and Healing for Struggling Parents*. These steps now appear as the guiding principles in all the books in the Setting Boundaries series from Harvest House Publishers. I mention them in many of the prayers in this book.

It is my prayer that God will continue to use these six steps to speak wisdom and truth into the lives of His children who long to grow closer to Him and to those they love.

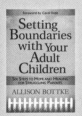

The Six Steps to SANITY

S—STOP my own negative behavior

A—ASSEMBLE supportive people

N—NIP excuses in the bud

I—IMPLEMENT a plan of action

T—TRUST the voice of the Spirit

Y—YIELD everything to God

My Angelic Support Group

For he will command his angels concerning you
to guard you in all your ways.

PSALM 91:11

I'm so thankful to You, dear Lord, for bringing me to this place of hope, healing, and sanity.

Thank You, too, for showing me the part I've played in the ongoing drama of my son's (daughter's) chaotic life. Lord, I've been running on the gerbil wheel of insanity for too long as I've tried unsuccessfully to change, fix, and rescue him (her). Help me break my habits of enabling and judging. Reveal to me the things You want me to change in my own life so I can pray more effectively for those I love. Let others hear You through the words I speak and see You in the way I live.

I can't do this on my own, Father, so I'm thanking You in advance for sending Your angels to stand guard and be my heavenly support group on earth. I praise Your holy name for the grace, mercy, and love You have given me.

The "A" Step in SANITY

Two are better than one,
because they have a good return for their labor:
If either of them falls down,
one can help the other up.

ECCLESIASTES 4:9-10

Jesus, I've made plenty of poor parenting choices. Please forgive me and create in me a pure heart and clear vision so I can walk confidently in Your will.

Lord, I praise You for the supportive people You send into my life. They help me look at my situations and circumstances objectively so I can respond to my adult child more rationally and less emotionally. Please help me overcome any silent shame or fear I may carry that keeps me from telling others the painful truth about my child. And please help me to listen with an open mind and heart and not to be judgmental when others share their stories.

I thank You in advance for guiding my head, heart, hands, and spirit to the lessons You will teach me daily from Your Word. Please help me to consistently utilize the SANITY Steps—not as temporary stopgap measures during times of crisis, but as the building blocks of a new way of life.

Accomplishment

Yield Fruit in Season

That person is like a tree planted by streams of water, which yields its fruit in season and whose leaf does not wither—whatever they do prospers.

PSALM 1:3

Heavenly Father, I thank You for the mighty work You're doing in the life and heart of my adult child. You know how difficult it has been for (name) to find his (her) calling in life. (Name) has struggled to get an education, juggle part-time jobs, and manage other responsibilities, and I'm filled with pride at the person he (she) has become. Even better, (name) is growing in faith and dependence on You along the way—that makes my heart sing and praise You in joy!

Lord, please show (name) how to align all his (her) actions with You. Open every door (name) should walk through and slam shut every door that he (she) shouldn't. Give him (her) peace about every decision. I pray that every season of (name's) life will be filled with success, prosperity, and abundant fruit as he (she) walks in obedience. May (name) experience the satisfaction of a job well done and bring glory, honor, and praise to Your holy name.

Accomplishment

Persevere and Receive the Promise

You need to persevere so that
when you have done the will of God,
you will receive what he has promised.

HEBREWS 10:36

Lord, I'm so thankful that when I'm weak, You are strong. As I've followed Your direction to set healthier boundaries with my adult child, the constant fears I once had have lessened. I'm growing stronger through Your Spirit in me. I'm now able to accomplish things that once seemed impossible, including praying for (name) in a new way.

When I tried to fix things my own way, the result was heartache and misery. By applying the "Y" step in SANITY and YIELDING—surrendering—my adult child to You, I've experienced a more joyful and fruitful relationship with him (her). Through Your wisdom and strength, I'm better able to prioritize my relationships without feeling guilty. What a wonderful feeling!

As I strive to be more like Your Son in my thoughts, actions, and deeds, my relationship with You fills my life with happiness. I know that as I persevere, You will pour out Your blessings on me and on my family.

The Nourishment of Your Strength

Even if I go through the deepest darkness,
I will not be afraid, LORD,
for you are with me.
Your shepherd's rod and staff protect me.

PSALM 23:4 GNT

Father God, I've lamented, grieved, and cried out to You about my drug-addicted child. I'm coming to You now to boldly ask for divine mercy and grace. (Name) needs help, but I don't know how to help or even if I should. I'm not a very good judge of what (name) really needs, but You are.

God, give (name) the light of Your love and the nourishment of Your strength. Please help her (him) to beat this life-threatening addiction. In Jesus's mighty name, please deliver my precious daughter (son) from the grip of Satan's influence. Release her (him) from this terrible bondage of addiction. Let (name) know what it feels like to breathe, walk, and exist in Your grace and mercy. Wrap Your loving arms around (name) as she (he) leaves the turbulence behind and steps into the healing flow of Your light and love.

Father God, help me to remember that I cannot change anything in (name's) life but You can change everything.

Total Surrender

*That is why we never give up. Though our bodies
are dying, our spirits are being renewed every day.*

2 Corinthians 4:16 nlt

God, my heart aches for the pain and suffering my adult child and his (her) loved ones are going through. (Name) is sick—I know alcoholism is a disease. I also know this dependence has been created by both (name's) choice to drink and by the addictive nature of alcohol itself.

This unhealthy dependence didn't happen overnight, and deliverance from this plague won't happen overnight either. But it won't happen at all if (name) doesn't admit that You are the only One who can restore his (her) life. In Jesus's name I pray for (name's) total surrender and complete restoration. Jesus, please convince (name) that with Your help, he (she) can conquer this disease and choose to stop drinking before it's too late.

Lord, help (name) experience the hope, healing, and freedom others are realizing as they put their trust in You and stop drinking one day at a time. Help (name) begin the life-changing journey that will lead to a new power, peace, happiness, and sense of direction. Help my child find serenity and sanity.

Jesus Saves

I am suffering and in pain.
Rescue me, O God, by your saving power.
PSALM 69:29 NLT

Lord, I've had enough of Satan's hold on my child's life! In Jesus's mighty name, I ask You to break the addiction that has captured my adult child's spirit, soul, and body.

Lord, I have faith in You and in Your Word, and I trust that You have a plan of healing and deliverance for my child. Fill (name) with confidence in Your saving power and hope for deliverance. Open (name's) eyes and break the bonds of denial holding him (her) captive. I pray for revelation of the root issues that feed (name's) addictions—and the supernatural power to conquer them. Merciful God, bless my precious son (daughter) with the courage and persistence to fight this addiction in Your name.

I can rejoice, knowing that every obstacle that comes before (name) will be destroyed and that he (she) will be delivered from this bondage of addiction. Empower (name) with the knowledge that he (she) can do all things through Christ, who gives him (her) strength. Father God, I love You and thank You for removing this stronghold of addiction.

Technology Trap

There is a way that appears to be right,
but in the end it leads to death.

PROVERBS 14:12

God, we've become enslaved to technological gadgets and apps. They were designed to make life easier, but they have opened the door to dangerous addictions. I can see the effect in my adult child's life. He (she) has contacts on the Internet that feed his (her) addictions. And (name's) mind is being corrupted by some of the garbage on the Internet.

Lord, I pray about all this. I pray that (name) may find hope on the Internet, not further destruction. Lead (him) her to find sites that will help him (her) overcome his (her) addiction. Keep him (her) from Internet contacts that are harmful...even if it means the loss of his (her) computer through a crash or some glitch. May his (her) computer become a tool in Your hands, not a force for evil in the hands of the enemy.

A Step in the Right Direction

Then your light will break forth like the dawn,
and your healing will quickly appear;
then your righteousness will go before you,
and the glory of the LORD will be your rear guard.

ISAIAH 58:8

God, thank You for getting my adult child into this inpatient treatment center. I pray for a covering of Your Spirit as (name) travels through the valley of addiction. May this be the last time (name) faces this demon. Keep (name) safe as the drugs (alcohol) leave his (her) body.

Be (name's) Comforter and Deliverer when all the emotions he (she) has stuffed away for years come rushing to the surface. Help (name) to be completely open and honest so he (she) can begin to heal. Let (name) willingly embrace the tools provided so he (she) is equipped to face anything when he (she) completes this detox program and returns home. I pray in Jesus's name that (name) will know that You are the only One who can fill the emptiness and bring lasting satisfaction. Give him (her) confidence that he (she) will never fall down when walking hand in hand with You.

Resist Enemy Influence

The eyes of the LORD range throughout
the earth to strengthen those whose
hearts are fully committed to him.

2 CHRONICLES 16:9

God, please heal the wounds and erase the scars that have provoked anger and discontent in (name's) heart. Set (name) free in Jesus's name from the negative emotions and painful memories that keep him (her) distanced from You and in bondage to toxic anger. Help him (her) resist the enemy's influence of any kind.

Give (name) the wisdom to know that he (she) can choose what goes into his (her) mind and eventually flows out of his (her) heart. Give (name) the desire and discernment to fill his (her) life with Your Word, worship, and the power of praise and thanksgiving.

Help (name) understand that he (she) will always be in a spiritual battle. Assure him (her) that the battle belongs to You and that he (she) can turn away from evil and turn all trials and adversities over to You. Thank You for Your promise that You will always come to the rescue and strengthen his (her) heart.

Strip Me of Anger

*Get rid of all bitterness, rage and anger, brawling
and slander, along with every form of malice. Be
kind and compassionate to one another, forgiving
each other, just as in Christ God forgave you.*

EPHESIANS 4:31-32

Father, my relationship with my adult child has been
strained for years, and our poor choices have left scars.
Lord, help me let go of all the anger I'm carrying—it's
such a heavy burden. I don't want to react impulsively
or emotionally because of pent-up anger. Help me
always to forgive and to release any resentment I have
toward (name).

As I've learned how to set healthy boundaries in
firmness and love, I've stopped running on the gerbil
wheel of insanity. I praise Your holy name for this freedom! Let this shift in my heart's perspective continue.
May I see all people through the lens of Your Spirit and
love each person unconditionally. Heal the wounds I've
endured and inflicted through the years, and help my
loved ones and me to put away this anger and pick up
Your love.

Remove the Chains

His anger lasts only a moment,
his goodness for a lifetime.
Tears may flow in the night,
but joy comes in the morning.

PSALM 30:5 GNT

I am so angry I could scream!

Just being able to say that is liberating. For the longest time I've tried to ignore these feelings, but I can't ignore this anymore. The fact is, I harbor more than a little resentment toward my adult child. I feel guilty and ashamed about this—and that makes me even more angry!

(Name) has lied to me, stolen from me, and disrespected, used, and abused me. (Name) has forgotten or ignored every birthday for years and most major family holidays. His (her) irresponsibility has caused significant money problems in my life.

God, I ask You to change my heart. Please help me find the right words, attitude, and actions to respond to (name) in a way that will free me from this anger. I know this isn't going to be an easy journey. I understand that forgiveness, redemption, and restoration is a process. Even so, I'm ready, Lord. I'm tired of carrying this anger.

Guard Your Heart

Above all else, guard your heart,
for everything you do flows from it.

PROVERBS 4:23

Jesus, You said that Your Word is like seed that bears fruit when it is planted in a humble and holy heart. Your Word tells us to protect our heart, for it is the wellspring from which everything flows. Father, I'm worried about the health of my adult child's heart. Lord, (name) has consistently given her (his) heart away to undeserving individuals and worldly influences that have leached away all nourishment, making it difficult for the seed of Your Word to take root and grow.

You give us spiritual boundaries, God, to keep us safe. Your commandments and promises provide us a hedge of security and protection. They help us guard our heart so Your Word can nourish our spirit and Christ can flow through us.

Pour out Your mercy on (name) and demonstrate Your great love and forgiveness. Show (name) that You alone can heal a broken and barren heart. Show (name) how deep Your love is—how valuable she (he) is to You.

Temptation

*No temptation has overtaken you except what is
common to mankind. And God is faithful; he
will not let you be tempted beyond what you can
bear. But when you are tempted, he will also
provide a way out so that you can endure it.*

1 CORINTHIANS 10:13

Lord, I see an inner battle waging in my adult child.
Resisting worldly temptation has never been easy for
(name). But the fight seems to be taking an increasing
toll. His (her) self-centered desires expose him (her) to
the lies and deceit of the enemy.

Lord, when (name) is tempted to instantly satisfy
his (her) selfish desires or to go with the flow and not
make waves, remind him (her) that true character is
all about doing the right thing when wrong things are
happening all around us.

Lord, help (name) to see the price we pay when
we don't live in honesty and integrity—when we deny
Your foundational principles. As the world around us
sinks further into a selfish lifestyle of sin and temptation, please give (name) the strength to stand firm in
Your Word and to speak Your truth with firmness and
love.

Change

Drown Out All Fear

*Make me truly happy by agreeing wholeheartedly
with each other, loving one another, and
working together with one mind and purpose.*

PHILIPPIANS 2:2 NLT

Lord, You've given me an awesome adult child, and I lift my hands high to You in praise. (Name) is a unique, quirky, and thoroughly lovable individual who can be of great service to You when all has been restored in her (his) life.

I pray for big changes to happen in both our lives as my daughter (son) finds hope in You. Drown out the fear of change—both in (name) and in me. Keep my thoughts positive as I praise and worship You for Your never-ending grace and compassion. I commit my life and the life of my precious adult child to You.

Keep me ever mindful that, in prayer, I can appropriate every promise You have given us in Your Word. Father God, I will continue to pray for (name) as long as I live. Help us both to continue to seek You in every decision we make. Give us wisdom to stand strong against the enemy, and grant us strength to meet every challenge.

Change

Seeing You in Me

See what great love the Father has lavished on
us, that we should be called children of God!
1 John 3:1

Lord, I thank You for helping me to look in the mirror and focus on the true person staring back at me. As I stop fixating on my adult child and all the chaos surrounding his (her) life, I'm able to see the person You created me to be. Thank You for giving me eyes to see Your Spirit living in me. For helping me to see that I, too, am important. For showing me that I'm a part of Your kingdom and Your family. For assuring me that no matter how many poor choices I make, You will still love me unconditionally and call me Your child.

Please help me to remember that when I remember who I am in You, I can respond to even the most chaotic situations with a peace that passes all understanding. Thank You in advance for the impact this shift in my perspective will make in all my relationships. I love You, Lord. Thank You for the love You are lavishing on me.

Walk This Way

Whether you turn to the right or to the left, your ears will hear a voice behind you, saying, "This is the way; walk in it."

ISAIAH 30:21

God, You know my heart. You know that I love (name) and that I really want to do the right thing, but sometimes I don't know what the right thing is. I need You to show me, to give me clarity.

I know that apart from You, I can do nothing of eternal value. And I believe I had to come to this realization of my powerlessness at exactly this time. Thank You for filling me every day with strength and power through Your Spirit. For assuring me that I can do all things as You strengthen me. I'm ready to change how I respond to the drama, chaos, and crisis that seem to consume (name's) life. I'm ready to find SANITY and set new and healthy boundaries with firmness and love.

Lord, I'm ready to do whatever is necessary to change my life. I trust that my adult child will also change as he (she) begins to see Your love through me.

New Eyes—New Perspective

Even before he made the world, God
loved us and chose us in Christ to be
holy and without fault in his eyes.

EPHESIANS 1:4 NLT

Lord, You know how hard I've tried to change and control my adult child—and how unsuccessful I've been. Too many times I've tried to rescue her (him) from the consequences of her (his) poor choices. I know that You created, love, and chose my child. You use everything for her (his) good, including the choices she (he) makes.

You have created a unique path for every one of Your children. My adult child's path is different from mine, and that's okay. But it isn't okay for me to force course corrections in her (his) path according to my will.

Help me to change my perspective on trials, to stay out of the way even when it's hard, and to watch You bring my adult child and me into our own destinies. I am filled with hope and joy knowing that You love us and will bring to pass whatever You have planned.

Show Me How to Love

*I have chosen him, so that he will direct his
children and his household after him to keep the
way of the LORD by doing what is right and just.*

GENESIS 18:19

Lord, I'm finding it hard to feel compassion for my adult child. There is so much anger, disappointment, and fear in my heart. Please let Your love flow through me, because I don't know how to compassionately love (name) on my own.

Father, I don't know how to be the firm and loving parent You want me to be, but I'm trusting You to show me the steps I need to take. Lord, it will take a miracle to change (name's) life. Perhaps I need a miracle to change my own life as well. Please strengthen my heart so I can show compassion and set healthy boundaries. Help me to live in a way that is pleasing to You, helpful to (name), and healthy for me. Help me to see what You see in my adult child. Help me to see (name's) real need and to respond in a way that reflects Your love.

God, Tell Me the Way to Go

*The LORD your God may tell us the way in which
we should walk and the thing that we should do.*

JEREMIAH 42:3 NASB

Lord, I have important choices to make concerning
my adult child. Please guide me in the choices I feel
You are calling me to make. I pray, Lord, that I won't
move ahead or fall behind You. Thank You for giving
me supernatural wisdom and discernment as You tell
me the way to walk and the thing I should do.

Father, I worship You today as the sovereign and
all-knowing God. You are the controller of all things.
I praise You, Lord, that You know what is best for my
family and me. Please grant me mercy and grace. Guide
me, dear Lord, as I make decisions regarding (name)
that will affect him (her) and our entire family.

Help me to rely on the "T" step in SANITY as I
TRUST in You and listen to Your still, small voice. I
thank You for hearing and answering this prayer. In
Jesus's name, I pray with holy confidence.

Choices

Trusting God with Our Choices

I sought the Lord, and he answered me;
he delivered me from all my fears.
Those who look to him are radiant;
their faces are never covered with shame.

Psalm 34:4-5

Compassionate heavenly Father, thank You for loving us and allowing us to make choices. We're not robots that simply do what we were programmed to do. Rather, You gave us the ability to choose. I confess that I haven't always asked You to help me make good decisions. Thank You for Your grace and mercy and for never leaving me to face the results of my choices alone.

Lord, I ask that my adult child will turn to You for guidance in making wiser choices than she (he) has made in the past—choices that honor You. Empower her (him) to use godly wisdom and not earthly passion when choosing friends, activities, and places to go.

Knowing I can't orchestrate all of my adult child's choices, I relinquish to You my desire to control. I put (name's) choices in Your hands and trust You with her (his) life. My ultimate choice is to trust in You, Lord.

Choices

What Time Is It?

There is a time for everything,
and a season for every activity under the heavens.

ECCLESIASTES 3:1

Lord, when circumstances don't make sense in my life, I've always been comforted by the story of Esther in the Bible. You allowed a young Jewish girl to become the queen of Persia and use her influence to save her people from annihilation. I'm inspired at how You showed Your love and grace through Esther. You showed how everything works together for Your grand purpose when we trust and obey You.

God, when I need to trust Your plan for my life, I think of the question put to Esther: "And who knows but that you have come to your royal position for such a time as this?" (Esther 4:14).

Lord, as my child faces trials, help him (her) choose wisely. Please guide (name) to make decisions rationally and not emotionally. Remind (name) that the choices we make can change the story of our lives. Help (name) to see that now is the time to make good choices.

A Heart of Compassion

Sing for joy, O heavens!
Rejoice, O earth! Burst into song, O mountains!
For the LORD has comforted his people
and will have compassion on them in their suffering.

ISAIAH 49:13 NLT

Lord, I pray for a heart of compassion toward my adult child just as You have compassion on the ones You love. It breaks my heart to see the choices (name) is making, and I'm helpless to empower him (her) to stand on his (her) own two feet. Remove from me all anger, unforgiveness, confusion, blame, and guilt. Please replace my broken heart with a compassionate heart.

I know I can't change what (name) does, but through Your Spirit, I can change myself and the choices I make. Help me remember that You have a divine plan for both of our lives. Please, Lord, let this be a season of pruning that will one day produce a bountiful harvest of fruitful blessings. As I stay in Your Word and seek You daily, I learn to reflect Your compassion and grace to the people You place in my life. Thank You for that.

A Fresh and Fragile Faith

Come to me, all you who are weary and
burdened, and I will give you rest.
MATTHEW 11:28

Lord, I want to rescue and protect my son (daughter) from his (her) trials. Yet I know that You have a sovereign plan and purpose for (name's) life—a plan I don't fully see. I trust that You have everything under control and that (name) is not alone on this current journey.

I know that (name) has mustard-seed faith. I believe that in his (her) pain and confusion, (name) cries out to You in prayer for relief. However, his (her) faith is fragile, and I don't want to jeopardize it by saying or doing anything that the enemy could use to drive a wedge between him (her) and You.

Please help me, Father, to have a compassionate heart and a patient spirit for my son (daughter) during this season of testing in his (her) life. Give me the wisdom and discernment to exhibit Your grace and mercy so he (she) will clearly see You in me.

Confidence

The New Me

*My heart is confident in you, O God; no wonder
I can sing your praises with all my heart!*
PSALM 108:1 NLT

What a joy it is to see my adult child walk in confidence and purpose! Thank You, dear Lord, for the mighty work You are doing in her (his) life.

I was afraid when You encouraged me to lay (name) at Your feet and stop my enabling habits. Thank You for showing me that as a helicopter parent, I was actually handicapping my child. By sheltering her (him) from the consequences of her (his) actions, I was also keeping her (him) from experiencing her (his) God-given destiny. I've also kept myself from experiencing my own destiny. Somewhere along the way I lost my own sense of purpose and my self-assurance.

I want to live a life that pleases You. To sing Your praises with all my heart and spirit. I know I'm valuable because I'm Your child. I love You, Lord, and I thank You in advance for directing me to the wisdom in Your Word that will help me grow into the person You want me to be.

Confidence

Wonderfully Made

*I praise you because I am fearfully
and wonderfully made.*

Psalm 139:14

Lord, I praise and thank You for holding my adult child in Your hands and keeping her (him) free from the bondage of fear and frustration. Give (name) the peace and confidence of never being alone, of knowing that You're walking alongside her (him) every step of the way. Remove any fear that (name) may have about the future and replace it with the healing confidence that comes when we completely trust in You.

Reveal to (name) how wonderfully You created her (him) to be. Give (name) a humble confidence in her (his) daily walk and the strength and wisdom to carry out what You have predestined for her (him) to be and do. Assure my adult child that You have deprived the enemy of the power to inflict permanent harm. May (name) walk in courage, joy, and love for others while developing a deep and growing hunger to want to know and love You more with every passing day.

Confidence

Finding Confidence in God's Love

*Set your hearts on things above, where Christ
is, seated at the right hand of God.*

COLOSSIANS 3:1

Father God, our world today shoots holes in our adult
children's confidence. Lord, only You can rebuild their
confidence on a sure foundation. Only You can encourage their hearts and help them know You love them
unconditionally.

May Your Holy Spirit convince (name) of Your
love, grace, and mercy. You don't repay us according to
our iniquities or treat us as our sins deserve. Instead, as
a perfect Father, You have compassion on each of us. As
far as the east is from the west, so far have You removed
the sins of those who fear You.

Please strengthen my adult child's heart, uphold
his (her) confidence, and help him (her) walk on the
sure foundation of Your love. Keep (name) from those
things that rob or damage his (her) self-esteem. Help
(name) to move forward, not living in regret but rather
living in freedom.

When our eyes are off our circumstances and on
You, we can walk in confidence. Please make that truth
real to my adult child right now.

Consequences

There Is No Escaping Pain

*The LORD disciplines those he loves, and he
punishes each one he accepts as his child.*

HEBREWS 12:6

God, these are some of the hardest lessons I've had to learn as Your child and as a parent: Pain is a necessary part of growth. Poor choices result in godly discipline. Unpleasant consequences can lead to encouragement and perseverance. I know this is a necessary and natural progression, Lord, but it isn't easy to accept when my own adult child is experiencing the painful consequences. I am tempted to ease his (her) pain.

That's why I come before You now, God. Strengthen my resolve to allow (name) to walk this road. I turn from my enabling behavior, which for so long has masqueraded as help.

I now realize that (name) doesn't need training wheels anymore. I can't continue to run behind (name) to protect him (her) from difficult situations and painful consequences. Help me to apply the "Y" step in SANITY and YIELD my adult child to You. When (name) stumbles in ways that break my heart, You can use the pain to build my adult child's character and courage.

Consequences

A World of Trouble

I have told you these things, so that in me you may have peace. In this world you will have trouble. But take heart! I have overcome the world.

JOHN 16:33

God, as my adult child endures the painful consequences of his (her) poor choices, I trust he (she) will learn to make better decisions. Lord, may he (she) not be battered or broken because of them. Help (name) to see that hitting rock bottom is not the end of life, but the beginning of a journey upward and into the miraculous power of Your light and love.

God, I humbly ask that (name's) painful consequences won't follow him (her) for the rest of his (her) life. Please supply (name) with the power to persevere in the face of all obstacles. Provide the unfailing trust that You have a plan and purpose for all pain. Instill the steadfast belief that any suffering here on earth will one day come to an end in heaven.

Consequences

Be Strong and Courageous

This is my command—be strong and courageous!
Do not be afraid or discouraged. For the LORD
your God is with you wherever you go.

JOSHUA 1:9 NLT

Lord, I'm consumed with fear for the safety of my adult child. After years of rebellion, addiction, and irresponsibility, the consequences of (name's) actions have sent him (her) into a tailspin.

Father God, do not let (name) become completely despondent because of the painful consequences he (she) is about to suffer. Let (name) rest in the assurance that whatever happens, You are in control, providing for all his (her) needs and loving him (her) with an unfailing love. Help him (her) face fear with Your grace, mercy, and love so he (she) can make the life-changing choice to stand tall and be courageous.

In Jesus's name I pray for the deliverance, redemption, and restoration my adult child needs. I ask You, dear God, to penetrate the heart of my son (daughter) and fill him (her) with the Spirit of truth and a supernatural courage to right the wrongs and to boldly face struggles in Your name and with Your power, grace, mercy, and love.

Speak Up or Shut Up?

From the mouth of the righteous
comes the fruit of wisdom,
but a perverse tongue will be silenced.

PROVERBS 10:31

Life is crazy, God! Sometimes I want to pack a bag, run away from home, and wait for You to fix everything. Sometimes I feel as if everyone around me is on a mission to push my buttons.

I'm completely baffled by a decision my adult child recently made. His (her) logic is utterly lost on me. In fact, when (name) shared this sudden brainstorm, it was all I could do not to scream, "Are you serious?" But I held my tongue. I'm learning at last that my unsolicited advice isn't nearly as effective as my prayerful silence.

However, Lord, I really need more direction on this issue. If I know this is a bad idea but don't say anything, what kind of parent does that make me? Should I share the wisdom of my experience only when I'm asked?

Father God, please help me to know whether it's time to speak up or shut up.

Consequences

A Rebellious Spirit

*In their hearts humans plan their course,
but the LORD establishes their steps.*

PROVERBS 16:9

Lord, I've made mistakes as a parent. In my desire to give (name) the things I did not have as a child, I over-indulged her (him). Fearful of damaging her (his) spirit, I failed to exercise healthy discipline. Because I didn't demonstrate that wrong actions have serious consequences, I inadvertently nurtured an arrogant and disrespectful adult—rebellious, self-serving, and self-destructive. I wish I had recognized what I was doing sooner, but I will not resign myself to the way things are. I have faith that change is possible.

Today, in Jesus's name and by His transforming power, I stand against rebellion and disobedience. I will no longer turn a blind eye to unacceptable, sinful behavior. I refuse to be held captive by my adult child's volatile emotions and destructive decisions.

God, please help me to consistently respond to (name's) choices from now on with firmness and love and in ways that bring glory and honor to You. Give me the words to assure (name) that I love her (him) but cannot—and will not—tolerate her (his) sin.

Courage

Make Me Courageous

Be strong and courageous. Do not be afraid or
terrified because of them, for the LORD your God goes
with you; he will never leave you nor forsake you.

DEUTERONOMY 31:6

Lord, please give me courage to follow through and stand strong in the new boundaries I put in place with my adult child. I love (name) so much, and it breaks my heart to watch him (her) go through trials again and again. However, I can see now that by enabling (name), I've contributed to these recurring downfalls. I've tried to fix the brokenness in (name's) life, but clearly, my ways don't work. Forgive me, Father, for the mistakes I made in the past. Help me to stop repeating them.

I ask in Jesus's name that (name) will receive supernatural courage to stand tall and accept the responsibility and consequences for his (her) choices. Give my adult child and me the courage to walk one step and one day at a time into the unknown, always remembering that You are leading us. You hold our future in Your hands. As we trust and obey You, victory will come.

Do Not be Discouraged

...but God is the strength of my heart.
Psalm 73:26

Dear Lord, I'm desperate for Your presence today. I trust in You alone for courage. I praise You for Your unconditional love.

Father, I bring my adult child before You today. (Name) is facing some serious consequences from past choices, and this time, no one is going to jump in and come to the rescue. I pray that the scales will fall from (name's) eyes and that he (she) will have the courage to stop running from reality and accept his (her) responsibility. I pray You will cause those involved to extend mercy and grace as they see his (her) willingness to stand up and be accountable.

Father, You are the strength of my heart. Please bring (name) and me peace and serenity today. Please continue to give me the wisdom and discernment to know what I should and shouldn't do in this situation. Thank You for giving me courage to follow through, Lord.

Hedge of Protection

*If you say, "The LORD is my refuge," and you make
the Most High your dwelling, no harm will overtake
you, no disaster will come near your tent. For he will
command his angels concerning you to guard you in
all your ways; they will lift you up in their hands, so
that you will not strike your foot against a stone.*

PSALM 91:9-12

Lord, every time the phone rings at night I freeze in terror. Although (name) no longer lives at home, I still worry. I still feel the urge to protect him (her) from the consequences of his (her) destructive choices and reckless living.

Lord, let every dark place in (name's) life be flooded with the light of Your truth so that nothing is hidden and everything is exposed. Show him (her) the danger of making poor choices. O God, may my precious son (daughter) repent of all sin and give his (her) life completely to You. Until that day, heavenly Father, I continue to pray for a hedge of protection around my child. Cover (name) with the blood of Jesus. May Your angels never leave his (her) side.

Danger

My Refuge

*Those who live in the shelter of the Most High will
find rest in the shadow of the Almighty. This I
declare about the LORD: He alone is my refuge, my
place of safety; he is my God, and I trust him.*

Psalm 91:1-2 NLT

Lord, the older I get, the more aware I become of the
collateral damage caused by insufficient boundaries.
God, help me remember that when I try to intervene
in my child's life, I do more harm than good. When
I try to fix things that only You can control, I almost
always suffer. So do my relationships.

Father, hold me tightly in Your arms so that when
I feel frustrated and hopeless, Your love will surround
me and lift my spirit from irrational, negative thoughts.
Help me keep my eyes on You, knowing that You're in
control, You have a plan already mapped out, and I can
keep myself from all kinds of danger if I just trust in
You. You keep me safe even when I don't realize it.

A Heavenly Life Preserver

My comfort in my suffering is this:
Your promise preserves my life.

PSALM 119:50

Lord, when horrible things happen, my adult child finds it hard to be resilient. (Name) has never been able to use healthy coping strategies and get the right care and support. This time, Lord, I'm afraid (name) has reached a place of unmanageable pressure, and without immediate intervention, something tragic might happen. (Name) has been so damaged by life, he (she) is too tired to go on and might consider opting out of life entirely.

I know that suicide is not Your will for (name). You have a unique purpose and a plan for (name), and this is not it. God, please do something in (name's) life now to prove how valuable he (she) is to You. Lord, keep (name) from doing anything harmful to himself (herself) or others.

God, help me share with (name) that he (she) isn't alone. Many people are hurting in the same way, feeling desperately alone and assuming no one understands their pain. And help (name) see that even when we're at the end of all our resources, You are here.

Dependence

An Instrument of Influence

Trust in the LORD with all your heart;
do not depend on your own understanding.
Seek his will in all you do,
and he will show you which path to take.

PROVERBS 3:5-6 NLT

Lord, I long for my adult child to develop a greater hunger for Your Word, a stronger love for others, and a more intimate relationship with You. I want so much for (name) to turn away from an unhealthy dependence on me and toward a healthy dependence on You. Please show me how to help make this transition happen in the most godly way possible. Help me to be a positive influence without being controlling.

God, You have revealed so much to me about Your grace, mercy, love, and power. You have blessed me with a sense of peace and hope. How I long for my child to experience You in the same way.

Lord, You are a powerful God. You can do powerful things. You offer me an inheritance—abundant gifts, blessings, and fruit that are available to me here and now, and life with You in heaven forever! Thank You, Lord—I praise and honor You today and always.

The Gift of Pain

The LORD has made everything for his own purposes.
PROVERBS 16:4 NLT

Thank You, heavenly Father, for being my wise and loving Teacher. I praise You for Your firm but gentle correction. As I continue to transition from self-reliance to God-reliance, I pray that I can become a parent of godly influence as I learn to make the most of my PAIN (Pause And Invite New feelings).

Thank You, Jesus, for helping me to pause and invite new feelings. For teaching me to depend on You to make everything new again—including my negative feelings. Thank You for giving me the strength to experience my painful feelings in the safety of Your healing love.

Father, please open the eyes of (name's) heart so she (he) can make the most of her (his) pain. I pray that You give her (him) the desire to please You and the willingness to depend on You as a kind and loving Teacher. Give (name) the supernatural insight to view pain from a new perspective. Help (name) to clearly see Your plan and purpose behind everything as she (he) comes to utterly depend on You.

I Will Strengthen You

Do not fear, for I am with you;
do not be dismayed, for I am your God.
I will strengthen you and help you;
I will uphold you with my righteous right hand.

ISAIAH 41:10

God, my son (daughter) needs You. (Name) is feeling broken and battered. Nothing I say or do seems to help. The hopelessness and despair (name) feels is causing him (her) to withdraw into a dark hole. If I feel powerless against this downward spiral of depression, I can only imagine how (name) feels.

Father, let Your love and grace shine in the darkness and provide hope and healing. Please help (name) make adjustments so he (she) can experience You in a deeper way. Remove any spirit of stubbornness or fear that keeps (name) from acknowledging You, and give him (her) a genuine willingness to be obedient to Your will and Word. Reveal to (name) that depression is not Your best for him (her). Assure him (her) that as he (she) pursues an intimate and obedient relationship with You, the veil of darkness will be replaced by a covering of Your compassion, character, and love.

Put Your Hope in God

Why, my soul, are you downcast?
Why so disturbed within me?
Put your hope in God,
for I will yet praise him,
my Savior and my God.

PSALM 42:5

Lord, in Your sovereign and holy name, I plead for my adult child's healing and deliverance. A dark cloud of despair is holding (name) hostage, and nothing I can do will help. Only Your power can save and deliver (name) from the bondage of painful memories, paralyzing fear, and post-traumatic stress.

God, You can do the impossible. You heal the sick, give refuge to the weary, and redeem lost souls. You can take the broken pieces of a tragic life and put them back together. Lord, I'm asking You to do whatever it takes to release (name) from this crippling depression and pervasive sense of hopelessness. Bring him (her) out of isolation and open doors to mental health care providers who can help. God, I thank You that my child is Your child as well and that You love him (her) even more than I do.

God Knows His Plans

*"For I know the plans I have for you," declares
the* LORD, *"plans to prosper you and not to harm
you, plans to give you hope and a future."*

JEREMIAH 29:11

Father, sometimes I don't know which way to go when I'm facing a fork in the road. Lately, the straight and narrow path seems to have eluded me. Still, my deepest desire is to walk in Your will.

Lord, thank You for promising that You will fulfill Your purposes for me, my adult children, and every member of my family. I praise You for Your amazing grace and for the plans You have for our lives today and in the future. Please give us clear direction concerning those plans. Shine Your light of truth on our paths. Deliver us from the power of any darkness that may keep us from walking in Your will.

Lord, can You increase my faith today? Can You assure me that I'm making the right choices? Help me to see not only the visible blessings but also the unseen, eternal things of God.

I love You, Lord, and praise Your holy name.

Direction

Show Me the Way

Your word is a lamp to my feet and a light to my path.
PSALM 119:105 AMP

Lord, (name) has struggled with school, work, roommates, finances, and finding her (his) purpose and passion in life. She (he) hasn't been able to find the right niche, to get a break. That's why I continued to help with financial resources year after year after year—until You convicted me that I was the one who really needed a major course correction. Thank You for showing me that it was time to let go of the tight grip I had on (name). That it was time for her (him) to depend on You rather than on me.

The transition hasn't been easy, but we're leaning heavily on Your wisdom, grace, mercy, and love as we enter this new season in our relationship. Help us to depend on Your Word and remain steadfast in our walk with You as we both pray for clear direction. Help us to follow Your priorities, not our own.

Though my precious daughter (son) and I walk different paths, I trust that You will guide us to the same destination—Your love.

The Next Right Thing

The road the righteous travel is like the sunrise,
getting brighter and brighter until daylight has come.

PROVERBS 4:18 GNT

Blessed are the cracked, for they let the light in.

God, my adult child's disabled brain cannot fix itself. But I'm trusting You for a breakthrough—may Your love pierce the dark places of my adult child's heart and mind and cause a miraculous change. Please help (name) to let Your light in through his (her) brokenness.

Lord, please prompt (name) to realign his (her) attitude, change his (her) perception, and get the professional help he (she) needs to move forward. Send a skillful professional with godly influence who can help (name) grieve the past, let the light in, and transition into a hopeful future. Give (name) the wisdom and strength to be a good steward of his (her) body and health. Empower my son (daughter) to boldly refuse to let any physical or mental limitations determine his (her) ability to be all You created him (her) to be.

A Painful Truth

*Do you not know that your bodies are temples of the
Holy Spirit, who is in you, whom you have received
from God? You are not your own; you were bought
at a price. Therefore honor God with your bodies.*

1 Corinthians 6:19-20

God, I can no longer deny the painful truth of my
adult child's mental and emotional disabilities. I can no
longer turn a blind eye to his (her) self-destructive irresponsibility or make excuses for unacceptable behavior.
Father, it grieves my heart that my adult child refuses
to accept responsibility for his (her) own physical and
emotional health.

(Name) is committed to maintaining a consistent
level of nicotine and caffeine in his (her) system, but he
(she) can't maintain a healthy balance of nutrition and
exercise. If he (she) would take his (her) medication consistently, several of his (her) issues would be addressed.

Lord, I can't force (name) to take care of himself
(herself). But I can't watch him (her) continue to self-
destruct either. Give me wisdom, God, as I continue
to yield (name) to You. Show me the next step. I need
guidance, and my child needs healing. Help us both,
O Lord.

I Am Willing

Observe the commands of the LORD your God,
walking in obedience to him and revering him.

DEUTERONOMY 8:6

Lord, You have called me to be diligent in Your Word and obedient to Your direction. Help me focus on Your commands and not on what my adult child is or isn't doing. Keep me from being led by my emotions so I can stand strong on Your Word. When the drama, chaos, and crisis in (name's) life threaten to spill over into mine, reveal to me Your good and perfect will. If Your direction is to be still and wait, give me the power to rest in You.

I thank You for the blessings that come as I heed Your firm and loving discipline and follow through even when I don't understand Your ultimate plan. I know that as I walk in obedience, You will bring me peace beyond my comprehension. Then I can be the kind of parent my adult child really needs. Your firm and loving discipline will flow through me, and Your spiritual truth and wisdom will flourish in me.

Father Knows Best

God's discipline is always good for us, so that
we might share in his holiness. No discipline is
enjoyable while it is happening—it's painful! But
afterward there will be a peaceful harvest of right
living for those who are trained in this way.

HEBREWS 12:10-11 NLT

God, You offer discipline not to punish us, but as a
Father who is correcting children He dearly loves. You
want to save us from the dangerous paths that lead
us astray. Lord, my adult child needs Your correction
more than ever as he (she) ventures further into darkness and wanders further away from You.

Today, in Jesus's name, I pray that (name) will
become desperate enough to accept Your loving discipline and do whatever You ask to change the course of
his (her) life. Holy Spirit, protect (name) from the evil
one, let the scales fall from his (her) eyes, and replace his
(her) stubborn heart of stone with a teachable heart of
flesh. Let (name) take that step of faith into Your open
arms of mercy and grace so You can carry him (her)
safely out of darkness and into the light of Your healing and hopeful love.

Divine Appointments

*Work willingly at whatever you do, as though
you were working for the Lord rather than
for people. Remember that the Lord will
give you an inheritance as your reward, and
that the Master you are serving is Christ.*

COLOSSIANS 3:23-24 NLT

God, our boomerang child is causing tension at home.
When he (she) needed to come home temporarily, we
welcomed him (her). But what began as a stopgap measure doesn't appear to be changing. (Name) needs to
start assuming more responsibility for personal and
household expenses. He (she) needs to feel the accomplishment that comes from hard work. God, my adult
child needs a job.

Lord, I pray for divine appointments to open up
for (name) as I encourage him (her) to actively pursue
employment. I pray for job opportunities that will enable
(name) to stand on his (her) own feet and walk in his
(her) gifting and purpose. Help me to balance love and
limits during this difficult season in (name's) life. Help
me to speak encouraging words that lift him (her) up
and don't tear him (her) down. Thank You, Jesus, for the
empowering work You are already doing in (name's) life.

Hard Work Develops Character

*Let us not become weary in doing
good, for at the proper time we will
reap a harvest if we do not give up.*

GALATIANS 6:9

Lord, help my adult child not to fear or refuse hard work. Help (name) to be diligent and responsible in the labor of his (her) hands. Let (name) feel the sense of accomplishment and personal satisfaction that comes from working hard. Give (name) the assurance that he (she) doesn't labor in vain.

Even more important, help (name) be willing to take direction from the wisdom in Your Word. Open (name's) eyes to see that hard work develops character. Let (name) feel a sense of achievement from a job well done, and show (name) what he (she) is truly capable of accomplishing when he (she) believes in, trusts, and follows You.

When Helping Hurts

Fathers, do not provoke your children to anger by the way you treat them. Rather, bring them up with the discipline and instruction that comes from the Lord.

EPHESIANS 6:4 NLT

Thank You, Lord, for opening my eyes to the ways I've enabled my adult child. It's painful to discover that in my desire to help, I may have handicapped (name) instead. Forgive me for my mistakes and help me continue to see the ways I need to change.

Keep all evil thoughts and feelings of blame, guilt, and anger away from me. What's done is done, and there's no undoing the mistakes I've made. Please help me forgive myself and make amends to those I've hurt by trying to fix things that were not my responsibility. Help me find hope and healing in my journey to be the person You want me to be. Strengthen me to live the life You would have me live. Help me fully trust You regardless of what happens.

And Lord, please teach me how to effectively pray for my child. Give me wisdom to understand the new parenting journey I must take.

I Will Keep Your Commands

*Oh, that their hearts would be inclined to fear me
and keep all my commands always, so that it might
go well with them and their children forever!*

DEUTERONOMY 5:29

Lord, I'm ashamed to admit how I've enabled my child
to avoid responsibility and escape the consequences of
his (her) actions. Rather than helping (name) grow into
a productive and responsible adult, I've made it easier
for him (her) to become even more dependent and irresponsible. Father God, please forgive me for my part in
the increasingly dysfunctional dynamic of our relationship. The conviction from Your Spirit to stop enabling
(name) has become too strong to ignore.

I'm ready to accept responsibility for my choices—
past, present, and future. This won't be easy, but I know
I can do it with You by my side. I'm not looking for a
quick fix, God. I'm ready to learn what it means to walk
in Your will. Please develop Your character in me so I
can reorient my life and keep it God-centered.

Building Bridges

*Brethren, I do not count myself to have apprehended;
but one thing I do, forgetting those things which
are behind and reaching forward to those things
which are ahead, I press toward the goal.*

PHILIPPIANS 3:13-14 NKJV

God, I can no longer pretend that my dysfunctional relationship with my adult child is normal. We seem to be unable to move beyond the pain of past choices. We harbor real and imagined hurts. Our conversations are often volatile, so we go for days without talking.

This destructive dynamic is not Your plan. Lord, it's time for this vicious cycle of enragement and estrangement to end, and I'm asking You to heal my family. Please help me know how I can get this process started. What can I say? What can I do?

I love my children, and I'm sorry for the part I have played in contributing to the chasm that has grown between us. Help us change our ways and begin living a fruitful family life. Please help me lead those I love in a new direction so we can begin building bridges and shortening the distance between us.

A Future Hope

Those who sow with tears
will reap with songs of joy.
Psalm 126:5

Lord, my feelings of pain and emptiness are sometimes overwhelming. I'm clinging to Your promise that one day my tears will give way to songs of joy.

Thank You for showing me that I can no longer accept responsibility for the negative and often dangerous choices (name) is making. Thank You for encouraging me to stop living on the gerbil wheel of insanity. That decision came at a great price—a painful estrangement from my child. Father, I know I made the right decision, but the separation between us still hurts. However, I choose to believe in my heart that this painful discord will lead to songs of joy.

Please build a healing bridge between us. I continue to hope. I continue to place Your Word deep in my heart and fully embrace Your plan for my relationship with my child—even if I don't always understand it. And I continue to keep my heart and arms open to welcome my precious son (daughter) home—on this side of heaven or the other.

Soul Improvement

"'If you can'?" said Jesus.
"Everything is possible for one who believes."
MARK 9:23

Lord, I recently watched some home-improvement programs on television. The common thread was the ability to visualize the restoration and the willingness to do the work to make the vision become reality.

Isn't that the story of life, God? The home-improvement shows reminded me of some people's soul-improvement stories. Lord, my adult child needs a soul-improvement restoration. Please renew (name's) spirit by placing a vision of restoration in his (her) heart. Bring godly people of influence into (name's) life to help him (her) complete the renovation.

So many things in life are causing (name) to become discouraged and weary. Please bring him (her) a fresh hope. Don't let him (her) lose heart. Thank You, God, for seeing the potential in (name's) life. Thank You for Your ability to restore a life damaged by years of neglect and abuse. Jesus, You are the Master Carpenter. By Your wounds we have been healed, and by Your blood we are set free. Thank You for a complete restoration of (name's) soul.

Do Not Be Afraid

Do not be afraid, for I am with you;
I bring your children from the east
and gather you from the west.

ISAIAH 43:5

Lord, I'm afraid for the life of my child. I'm afraid of the consequences of his (her) actions. Please help me feel a peace that surpasses all understanding—I want so desperately to know that comfort. I don't want to live with this heavy weight of fear on my heart, so I'm asking You to please take this burden from me.

Father God, I pray for You to open (name's) eyes to the truth about the road he (she) is traveling and where it leads. Reveal Your plan and purpose for (name's) life. God, will You please send someone of spiritual influence into my adult child's life who will give him (her) the godly direction he (she) so desperately needs? And Lord, please help me know how to deal with my fear in a healthy way.

What God Has Not Given

God has not given us a spirit of fear, but of
power and of love and of a sound mind.

2 TIMOTHY 1:7 NKJV

God, some nights I go to sleep afraid—concerned about my adult child's most recent drama. I'm so thankful when she (he) calls to stay in touch. But I'm always so worried and on edge after our conversations, that a part of me doesn't want to answer the phone when the caller ID shows her (his) name. I'm weary of being filled with fear about (name's) choices.

Lord, help me to trust completely in Your perfect plan. I know that nothing is impossible with You. Today, I pray I will grow deeper in my faith so as to cancel out all FEAR (False Events Appearing Real). I know that You are my Helper, and I will not fear what man—or false events—can do to me. Teach me how to respond differently to my daughter (son) the next time I get an unsettling call. I will not fear attacks of the evil one, who roams like a roaring lion, because Your Word dwells deep in my heart.

All You Can Hold

Give to others, and God will give to you.
Indeed, you will receive a full measure, a
generous helping, poured into your hands—
all that you can hold. The measure you use for
others is the one that God will use for you.

LUKE 6:38 GNT

Lord, I'm desperate. For so long I've pretended that my relationship with my adult child is just a little bent out of shape, but the truth is, it's horribly broken. And I'm finding it very hard to forgive and forget the pain his (her) choices have caused me and my family.

Lord, please heal my heart. Help soften the sharp edges of the painful memories that so often overtake me. Fill me with the light of Your love and the healing power of the Holy Spirit. Help me to move forward and not look backward. Jesus, thank You for giving me the strength and wisdom to forgive and put the past behind me. Thank You for the ability to set and keep healthy, God-honoring boundaries that reflect the character of Christ.

Release the Burden

*When you are praying, first forgive anyone
you are holding a grudge against, so that your
Father in heaven will forgive your sins, too.*

MARK 11:25 NLT

Lord, You know all about my broken relationship with my adult child. You know how much pain, anger, and mistrust exist between us. I know that for complete healing to ever come, both of us must forgive. God, will You please help us to release our burdens of hurt? Help us forgive one another and let go of the disappointments of the past.

Give us the strength and wisdom to reach deep down and acknowledge that although we may have failed in some areas, we are not failures. We can do all things through Christ, who gives us strength—and "all things" includes restoring our fragile relationship. Dear God, let Your love overshadow every negative thought as we release the past and walk boldly in Your generous grace and forgiving love. In Jesus's name I declare today that the enemy can no longer have a foothold in our relationship through unforgiveness. And I pray that You will open doors of opportunity for this restoration to heal us both.

No Record of Wrongs

He is so rich in kindness and grace that
he purchased our freedom with the blood
of his Son and forgave our sins.
EPHESIANS 1:7 NLT

Father, my adult child is holding on to so much pain, rejection, and abuse from the past. His (her) unhealthy need for retribution and vindication is like a festering wound in his (her) heart.

You want us to be generous with our love, grace, and forgiveness. But we can't give away what we don't have, and right now, (name) isn't open to receiving these things from You. However, I believe in miracles, and I'm praying for You to do a miraculous work in (name's) life, starting now. Dear God, I pray my adult child can find freedom from the horrible bondage of an unforgiving heart. Help (name) see that the process of righting all the oppressive wrongs begins in his (her) own heart.

We are never more like Jesus than when we forgive someone, including ourselves. Show my adult child what Jesus would do, and give (name) the strength and courage to do it with praise and thanksgiving.

A Secure Identity

*Let the peace of Christ rule in your hearts, to which
indeed you were called in one body. And be thankful.*
COLOSSIANS 3:15 ESV

God, my adult child's heart is filled with envy, inferiority, and insecurity. She (he) thinks she (he) doesn't have value. Lord, I ask You to help (name) stop making these hurtful comparisons. Please set her (him) free from wanting what other people have and open her (his) eyes to the many gifts and blessings You have graciously provided.

Help (name) feel secure in Your love, O God. Show (name) ways to stop the destructive habit of comparing herself (himself) to others. Help (name) to reject the lies of the enemy and to find her (his) true identity in the truth of Scripture. I pray in Jesus's name that all doors to envy and inferiority be slammed shut. Let the peace of Christ rule in her (his) heart, and give her (him) wisdom and strength to see her (his) incredible value and worth to You.

Genuine Humility

For everything in the world—the lust of the
flesh, the lust of the eyes, and the pride of life—
comes not from the Father but from the world.

1 JOHN 2:16

Lord, my adult child seems to walk through one trial after another without seeing the part he (she) is playing in the drama. I fear that if (name) is not stripped of all pride, arrogance, and irresponsibility and brought to his (her) knees, he (she) will continue to think he (she) is indestructible. You and I both know that isn't true.

I'm helpless to influence (name) in this area, and I ask that You do whatever it takes to humble my adult child and free him (her) from this bondage. I know that when we're full of pride, we keep ourselves from Your love. But when we are truly humble and put others before ourselves, we find inner peace. I pray that You will open (name's) eyes so that he (she) can change in this area.

Lord, I ask You to give (name) wisdom and discernment so he (she) can make heartfelt changes and receive all the blessings You are just waiting to pour out.

Pressing Forward

*Not that I have already obtained all this, or have
already arrived at my goal, but I press on to take
hold of that for which Christ Jesus took hold of me.*

PHILIPPIANS 3:12

Lord, please help (name) fan into flame the gift of faith
You have placed in his (her) heart. May (name) embrace
a brand-new beginning, determined that there is no
room in his (her) future for the sins of the past. (Name)
has wasted fruitless years mourning and regretting a
past that cannot be changed. Help him (her) forget
what is behind and strain toward what is ahead. Let my
son (daughter) break free from his (her) past.

I pray that (name) will let go of yesterday's sins and
come to realize that his (her) life can change in miraculous ways when he (she) repents and starts heading in
the right direction. I thank You in advance for opening
the eyes of (name's) heart to see that You are the Healer
of all damaged souls and broken places. That with faith,
hope, and love, he (she) can begin again and press on
to take hold of that for which Christ Jesus took hold
of him (her).

Friendship

Remove the Influence of Sin

*Do not be misled: "Bad company
corrupts good character."*

1 CORINTHIANS 15:33

Lord God, I'm concerned about the influences in my
adult child's life. I know (name) isn't completely inno-
cent, but there's no denying that when he (she) spends
time with the right friends, he (she) experiences decid-
edly less drama.

Surely (name) doesn't want to infect his (her) life
with people of bad character, questionable morals, and
illegal motives. Could it be that he (she) really doesn't
see the forest for the trees—that in his (her) desire to
have friends and not be alone, he (she) is unable to tell
good from bad? Please, Lord, give (name) a desire to
fill those lonely spaces and empty places with wisdom
from Your Word and not the influence of sin.

God, I pray for (name) to be filled with fresh knowledge and understanding concerning friendship. Please
bring people into (name's) life who can influence him
(her) in positive ways. Give (name) the ability to differ-
entiate between good and bad influences.

Fruitfulness

This Kind of Fruit

*The Holy Spirit produces this kind of fruit in our
lives: love, joy, peace, patience, kindness, goodness,
faithfulness, gentleness, and self-control.*

GALATIANS 5:22-23 NLT

God, I desperately want to exhibit the fruit of the Spirit.
I pray I will be courteous, considerate, gentle, and full
of compassion with those I meet. I long to show others
the same love You have shown me. I admit I have not
always been successful in this, especially with (name).

God, I struggle to say yes with honest authenticity
and no with firmness and love. I often find myself saying and doing things I really don't want to say or do—
simply because I don't want to rock any boats, hurt
anyone's feelings, or cause anyone problems. I do what
I think others expect of me. Because of that, I've been
carrying around a lot of pent-up frustration, anger, and
resentment at the difficult people in my life. No wonder my life wasn't producing wholesome fruit.

Thank You for helping me to set healthy boundaries
with my adult child, release my feelings of resentment,
and bear good fruit.

Growing the Roots of Wisdom

I am the true vine, and my Father is the gardener.
He cuts off every branch in me that bears no
fruit, while every branch that does bear fruit he
prunes so that it will be even more fruitful.

JOHN 15:1-2

God, sometimes my precious adult child wants to follow Your will but has difficulty discerning what that is. I pray that she (he) would ask You daily, "Lord, is this what You want for me?"

Father, I pray for (name) to be fruitful and prosperous in every area of life—work, school, relationships, finances, or any daily responsibility. Remove all fear from her (his) mind and replace it with confidence and courage, trusting fully that she (he) is able to accomplish anything with You. In Jesus's mighty name, I ask You to dispel anything holding (name) back from the greatness You have instilled in her (him).

May (name) grow in wisdom and discernment through Your Word. Let Your priorities guide her (his) journey. I pray that (name) will bear abundant fruit through Your Spirit.

A Real and Tangible Way

I will plant her for myself in the land; I will show
my love to the one I called "Not my loved one." I
will say to those called "Not my people," "You are
my people"; and they will say, "You are my God."

HOSEA 2:23

Lord, an emptiness is growing inside my adult child, a darkness and fear I can see in her (his) eyes. Lord, You are so magnificent, so full of mercy and grace, and I ask in Your holy name that You would lift (name) up out of the pit of loneliness and fill her (him) with Your amazing love. Open the eyes of (name's) heart to see Your beautiful Spirit. I can't provide everything she (he) needs, but You can do more than I could ever imagine.

You provide strength for the weak, comfort for the brokenhearted, healing of all wounds, and refuge for the lost. Your love covers a multitude of sins. Show (name) Your love in a real and tangible way. Thank You for the work You are doing right now in (name's) heart, spirit, and mind.

Teach Me Your Love

I have loved you with an everlasting love;
I have drawn you with unfailing kindness.

JEREMIAH 31:3

Lord, I've been selfish in my love for my adult child. I've sought for years to meet (name's) needs by coming to his (her) rescue during difficult times. But You do some of Your best work in times of trial, shaping character and growing a person's faith. You were trying to stretch and strengthen my adult child, but I was only making him (her) more dependent on me and less on You. Please forgive me for sabotaging (name's) emotional and spiritual growth with my own selfish desires to rescue him (her). You're the Savior—I'm not.

Dear Jesus, I want to love the way You love. Help me align my desires with Yours. I come to You with arms wide open. I empty all of myself so that I may be consumed with Your everlasting love. Pour Your love into me and let it overflow, touching everyone around me.

Please Open a Door

*"What no eye has seen, what no ear has heard, and
what no human mind has conceived"—the things
God has prepared for those who love him—these
are the things God has revealed to us by his Spirit.*

1 CORINTHIANS 2:9-10

Father, as I pray for my adult child today, I find myself thinking about how poorly we communicate—and how much I would like that to change. I raised this child, but years of rebellion, addiction, and anger have built walls around both our hearts. I'm thankful we can talk at all, Lord, but I know You want more for us.

God, I'm asking You today to open doors to healthy communication so I can stop walking on eggshells around (name) and feeling as if I'm intruding. Lord, please give me the words to lovingly penetrate (name's) defenses of anger and mistrust. Give me wisdom to speak in kindness and love. Help me, Jesus, to learn how to talk to my adult child in a way that brings You honor and glory. Thank You for loving us and beginning to restore our relationship.

Receiving His Unfailing Love

See what great love the Father has lavished
on us, that we should be called children
of God! And that is what we are!

1 John 3:1

Thank You, heavenly Father, for reassuring Your children of Your generous love. You are not stingy with Your love, but continue to lavish Your love, mercy, and grace on us. Thank You for being a perfect and compassionate Father. Help me to always remember how much I am loved.

Father, I pray that my adult child would recognize and relish the power of Your unfailing love. Let Your love become so real that (name) feels enveloped by it. Help me reflect Your unchanging love as I relate to him (her). Pour out Your love through me as I deal with challenging situations. Give me strength to be firm and wisdom to set appropriate boundaries. You know what's best for us. In the same way, give me discernment to know when to give help and when to back off. Help (name) to be certain of my love even when I say no. Most importantly, help me to show him (her) a glimpse of what Your love looks like.

God Is Love

*We know and rely on the love God has
for us. God is love. Whoever lives in love
lives in God, and God in them.*

1 John 4:16

Lord, I'm watching my grandchildren struggle as they deal with their parents' sins, and I feel helpless. Help me know what to say to them and to my adult child as he (she) tries to put back together the pieces of his (her) broken heart and dreams. Give me wisdom and discernment so I can speak words of love and encouragement when these storms batter his (her) spirit. Help me to be the voice of calm and loving assurance that will enable him (her) to see Your love and to trust that You will never leave him (her).

Comfort my precious little grandchildren with a powerful heart knowledge they can carry forever—that if You bring them to it, You'll get them through it, regardless of what it might be. You are in their lives for the long haul, and You will always and forever love them unconditionally.

Grandchildren

At Wits' End

They were at their wits' end.
Then they cried out to the LORD in their trouble,
and he brought them out of their distress.

PSALM 107:27-28

God, I thought my parenting responsibilities were behind me. However, my grandchildren are suffering from my own adult child's irresponsible behavior. I can no longer be a spectator as my grandchildren are continually pulled into the drama of my adult child's dangerous addiction and dysfunction. Sadly, my daughter (son) is becoming increasingly incapable of being responsible for her (his) children's physical, emotional, and financial needs. I fear for their safety and their future.

Lord, I don't know what to do, but I must do something. Please help me. I'm so confused—I don't even know how to pray! Please guide my steps as I decide what must be done. Show me in a way that removes all doubt what actions You want me to take. Help me remain rational and not emotional as I face the consequences of my decisions.

Father God, please keep my grandchildren safe. And please deliver (name) from the demons of addiction and self-destruction that hold her (him) in bondage.

Speak the Truth in Love

*Now that by your obedience to the truth you
have purified yourselves and have come to
have a sincere love for other believers, love
one another earnestly with all your heart.*

1 Peter 1:22 GNT

Lord, I know that You reveal Your love to us through our relationships. I want to make a difference in my adult child's life, but (name) needs other faithful and caring friendships too. Please help (name) understand that the quality of her (his) friendships will help determine the quality of her (his) life. Give (name) wisdom and discernment when choosing friends.

Help (name) to set healthy boundaries in all her (his) relationships. Guide (name) to apply the "T" step in SANITY and TRUST the voice of the Spirit when she (he) comes to You in prayer about relational challenges. Let (name) grow in character as she (he) navigates the sometimes rough waters of communicating with friends, co-workers, and neighbors. Jesus, please send godly people into (name's) life who will be positive influences and who will speak the truth in love.

Guidance

A New Season

Trust in the LORD with all your heart. Never rely on what you think you know. Remember the LORD in everything you do, and he will show you the right way.

PROVERBS 3:5-6 GNT

Lord, when did life get so complicated? When did the lines between helping and hurting get so blurred? Why is it so hard to discern whether my choices are empowering or enabling (name)? As my perfect and loving Father, please show me how to be an effective parent.

The storms of life have taken their toll on my confidence. Today I find myself looking more in the rearview mirror at my past choices and less on the road ahead, where new choices await. Sometimes I question my actions, my direction, and even my purpose.

But I never question You, Lord, or Your love for me and my family. I know I can do all things when I walk with You. God, please reveal Your will for this new season in my life. As Your child, I humbly ask for Your strength, wisdom, and guidance. Help me be a parent who walks the talk.

A Hunger to Know You

Man is born to trouble,
As the sparks fly upward.
But as for me, I would seek God,
And to God I would commit my cause—
Who does great things, and unsearchable,
Marvelous things without number.

JOB 5:7-9 NKJV

Lord, I pray that my adult child may hunger to know You like never before. I pray for a deep conviction and healing tears that wash away pain from the past, reveal clarity in the present, and bring abiding hope for the future. I pray that You will remove any fear, anger, envy, and unforgiveness from (name's) heart that could prevent him (her) from taking that step of faith into Your redeeming love.

Father, (name) needs You now. On behalf of my precious son (daughter), I beg You to bathe every step (name) takes in the light of Your glorious love, grace, and mercy. Guide his (her) ways wherever he (she) turns. Lord, I pray that (name) may know the abundant blessings You pour out on those who seek Your face and walk in Your ways. Thank You for doing great and marvelous things on our behalf. What a gift, what a blessing!

Guilt

A World of Regret

Godly sorrow brings repentance that leads
to salvation and leaves no regret, but
worldly sorrow brings death.

2 CORINTHIANS 7:10

Lord, I remember the godly sorrow that helped me turn around and begin a new life in Christ. Being convinced of my sinful actions and attitudes wasn't easy. I'm painfully aware of the parenting mistakes I made. Sometimes I acted out of ignorance, but other times I knew better and simply ignored the still, small voice of warning.

I know that repentance leads to freedom and release from guilt. Thank You for helping me to make new choices that will change my life and my relationships with those I love. But there's a problem, God. False guilt is corroding my spirit. I feel as if I'm losing ground as I dwell on the past, focus on my failures, and maintain unreasonable expectations. One minute I can be feeling the sun-kissed glow of Your salvation, and the next I'm being kicked in the gut with self-condemnation, shame, and regret. Lord, I need Your help. Please give me clarity of mind and heart to accept true Holy Spirit conviction but to reject false guilt and fear.

Guilt

Cast Out Fear

Your faith has saved you; go in peace.
LUKE 7:50

Lord, please deliver me from the uncertainty and confusion I feel concerning my adult child. You are my strength and my shield, and I trust in Your Word. I know it's time to release (name) to You and not hover over her (him). (Name) needs to learn problem-solving skills and accept responsibility for her (his) actions. But my heart aches when I see her (him) in pain and struggling, especially when I know I could fix the problem.

I confess that my helping hasn't always been truly helpful, and that's why I'm torn. I want to be an obedient child and follow Your Holy Spirit's guidance. But how can I apply the "Y" step in SANITY and YIELD (name) to You without being smothered by feelings of guilt and fear should things go wrong? Lord, will You please show me Your perspective on my circumstances? Father, please reveal the truth through Your Word and give me peace as I learn how to love my adult child with open arms.

Healing

No Room for Doubt

*The LORD makes firm the steps
of the one who delights in him.*

PSALM 37:23

God, my heart is breaking. My adult children and their problems have become ever-present wounds that never seem to heal. I know You have provided a way for us to find hope and healing. Lord, I need You to show me that way.

Father, please help me develop a proactive action plan, something that will help me to get off the gerbil wheel of insanity. Please reveal that plan to me so clearly I have no doubt as to what I'm supposed to do. I know You give strength to the weary and increase the power of the weak, and I ask for that strength and power now.

I delight in You, Lord, and I thank You in advance for making my steps firm. Thank You for giving me insight and direction and for filling me with peace.

Keep Growing

*I pray that your love will overflow more and
more, and that you will keep on growing
in knowledge and understanding.*

PHILIPPIANS 1:9 NLT

Lord, I want to make communication with You a vital part of my daily existence and to develop an intimate relationship with You. However, I'm often consumed with rescuing other people in my life, especially my adult child. I always seem to be tempted to fix some drama, chaos, or crisis in (name's) life.

How do I know when to say yes and when to say no? How do I know whether my adult child needs prayer alone or also some firm accountability? When should I carry his (her) burdens, and when should he (she) carry his (her) own? Lord, sometimes I spend more energy focusing on the dysfunctional relationships in my life than I do on the healthy ones, especially my relationship with You. Can You please open the eyes of my heart to understand this anomaly? Help me to maintain my relationship with You as the main priority in my life.

Healing

A Tender Heart

The angel of the LORD encamps around those
who fear him, and he delivers them.

PSALM 34:7

Lord, how glorious it is to have emotions! Our emotions are part of what makes us human beings. They signal danger and prompt us to act or run away. They motivate us to meet our goals, needs, and desires. They can also reveal what's happening inside us.

But, Lord, my adult child has become a slave to her (his) emotions. Thank You, Father, for creating (name) with a tender heart and gentle soul. We are all born with God-given emotional needs for love, significance, and security. However, (name's) unfiltered emotions often cut through her (his) heart like a tornado cuts through a town. Please give (name) the wisdom and strength to calm her (his) emotional storm and balance her (his) emotions with rational thinking.

God, remove any unhealthy motivations that keep (name) on an emotional roller coaster. Please motivate her (him) to seek godly professional help, unpack the emotional baggage, and find a healthy balance in life.

Healing

Releasing Pain

I will instruct you and teach you
in the way you should go;
I will counsel you with my loving eye on you.

PSALM 32:8

Lord, many of us are casualties of less-than-perfect childhoods. However, that doesn't mean we're destined to live forever in the shadow of our past. We can work through the deep internal struggles and emotional messes we haven't wanted to address. Despite our past, we can still become confident, optimistic, and hopeful people.

Father, I'm sensing that my adult child hasn't been able to address some of those internal struggles. You know what they are, and You can heal them with Your love and grace. Please help (name) find the underlying cause of these heart issues and begin releasing the pain. I pray for a person of influence and experience to come into (name's) life and help him (her) dig down to the root of the issue and explore his (her) emotions, motivations, and needs. Help (name) break the bondage of the past and discover the extraordinary blessings that come from a relationship with You in the present and for eternity.

Healthy Life and Soul

Behold, I will bring to it health and healing,
and I will heal them and reveal to them
abundance of prosperity and security.

JEREMIAH 33:6 ESV

Lord, I'm concerned about (name's) physical, emotional, and spiritual health. God, please relieve the heavy burdens in his (her) life. Help him (her) to apply the "S" step in SANITY and STOP his (her) detrimental behavior. Help him (her) to see the hurtful effects of these actions, and show him (her) how to take care of his (her) health now.

Help (name) see the importance of taking care of his (her) body, soul, and spirit. Please give me wisdom and discernment so I can know how to share my concern with (name) without causing him (her) to become exasperated or discouraged.

Lord, I love You, and You know how much I love my adult child. Thank You in advance for the healing You are going to bring to (name's) life.

Restored to Health

*Beloved, I pray that all may go well
with you and that you may be in good
health, as it goes well with your soul.*

3 JOHN 1:2 ESV

Lord, I thank You for bringing health to my body and to my relationships. I'm enjoying a new freedom now that I've begun to apply the Six Steps to SANITY in the challenging relationships in my life. Giving myself permission to take care of my own mental, physical, and spiritual health, and releasing all the stress of having to fix everything and everyone—these have added years to my life and rejuvenated my whole being. When I began to consistently apply the "Y" step in SANITY and YIELD my adult child fully to You, I felt as if the sun had broken through a cloud of darkness.

Now that I'm connected to You and focused on Your plans for me, I have an abundance of peace and happiness. Your Word sustains me, and I'm filled with hope and thanksgiving. I like the new person You are molding me to be!

I Am God's Temple

Don't you realize that all of you together are the
temple of God and that the Spirit of God lives in you?
God will destroy anyone who destroys this temple.
For God's temple is holy, and you are that temple.

1 CORINTHIANS 3:16-17 NLT

Lord, I've prayed for my adult child's protection, but now I'm the one who needs help. I've become physically and emotionally sick with worry about (name's) poor choices. My heart is broken, my spirit is bruised, and my body is sending me warning signals I can no longer ignore. I haven't treated my own body as Your temple. I repent, Lord—thank You for forgiving me.

Thank You, too, for reminding me that I need to take care of myself. In my misguided desire to rescue others, I sometimes forget that Your plan for me is separate from Your purpose for my adult child.

Lord, I so appreciate the healing You're doing in my life. Help me, Jesus, to let go of what's behind, to set new and healthier boundaries with firmness and love, and to look to the future with hope.

Until the Storm Is Past

*O God, have pity, for I am trusting
you! I will hide beneath the shadow of
your wings until this storm is past.*

PSALM 57:1 TLB

Lord, I come to You during a difficult time. Please speak deep within my spirit as I trust in You.

Father, You know my adult child has strayed far from You. Please surround my prodigal loved one with Your mighty angels. Protect (name) from the attacks of the evil one and from anyone or anything that would come against him (her). Shelter (name) with Your protective wings until this storm is past. Cover (name) with the blood of Jesus and keep my precious child safe.

Father, I know that (name) believes in You, and I hold fast to his (her) confession of Jesus Christ as Lord and Savior.

I am reminded that everyone knows someone who is running from You. I pray, dear Lord, for all those whose hearts are breaking like mine today. Let them hide with me beneath Your sovereign love, grace, power, and mercy. Let them join me in confidence that Your light will shine through the dark clouds.

Help During Crisis

Whatever It Takes

I will win her back once again.
I will lead her into the desert
and speak tenderly to her there.
I will return her vineyards to her
and transform the Valley of Trouble
into a gateway of hope.

HOSEA 2:14-15 NLT

Heavenly Father, You are so mighty and powerful. You can lift us from the pit and bring us into the light of Your love and Spirit. I'm calling out to You now in desperation. My adult child is completely out of control. (Name) is spiraling downward in self-destructive behavior.

In Jesus's name I pray that (name) will see his (her) bondage to sin and overcome it. I pray for deep conviction that will bring (name) to his (her) knees—to a desperate and humbling place of total surrender to You. God, You are the only One who can save (name). Please do whatever it takes. I will stay out of the way so You can work in him (her). I'm not his (her) Savior—You are. You have called each of us for Your own purpose. Father, please empower (name) to become the beautiful child You created him (her) to be.

Quiet the Raging War

The righteous cry out, and the LORD hears them;
he delivers them from all their troubles.
The LORD is close to the brokenhearted
and saves those who are crushed in spirit.

PSALM 34:17-18

In the mighty name of Jesus, I pray against suicidal thoughts in my adult child's mind. Lord, keep Your hand on (name), and don't let him (her) fall prey to the lies of the enemy. Surround my precious son (daughter) with a hedge of protection that no evil can penetrate. Free him (her) from feelings of depression or hopelessness.

Reveal to (name) that You give us new life. Remind my child that suicide is Satan's counterfeit solution and that You never intended it for us. Help (name) to know that when life's burdens seem too heavy bear, he (she) can call people who are ready and willing to help him (her) regain perspective. Father God, please subvert any impulse for (name) to harm himself (herself). Quiet the raging war in his (her) spirit and provide a way out so he (she) can stand strong. Let Your light shine in the darkness.

At the End of the Rope

Discipline your children,
and they will give you peace;
they will bring you the delights you desire.

PROVERBS 29:17

Lord, how can I set boundaries with our adult daughter (son) when my spouse is the enabler? He (she) gives our child money, access to the car, and other material needs and always has an excuse for our daughter's (son's) negative and irresponsible behavior. My spouse doesn't see the problem.

Lord, I'm at the end of my rope. I just can't live this way any longer. I'm convinced that our child's behavior and my spouse's responses are wrong. I don't know what to do. We've spent so much time and energy caught up in the chaos of our child's life that we've neglected our own lives. Help us take the spotlight off our daughter (son) and focus it instead on our relationship. Lord, this frightens me because I'm not sure my spouse has any desire to shift our priorities.

God, please show me how to communicate with my spouse in a proactive way. Teach us how to honor You, help our adult child, and improve our own relationship.

Help!
My Child Has Been Arrested

The Holy Spirit helps us in our weakness. For example, we don't know what God wants us to pray for. But the Holy Spirit prays for us with groanings that cannot be expressed in words.

ROMANS 8:26 NLT

God, my adult child needs help that I'm unable to give. I'm too weak to do anything but pray. And this time, maybe that's for the best.

(Name's) choices have finally caught up with him (her), and the long-term legal ramifications are serious. I have been afraid this would happen, so I have always rushed to (name's) rescue with bail money and legal resources. But not this time. This time things are different as I willingly step back to let Your Holy Spirit work.

(Name) is not alone—You are there. I can't solve this problem, but You can. Nothing is impossible for You. Please keep my son (daughter) safe. In this situation, may (name) come to his (her) senses, start making better choices, and learn to depend on Your presence in his (her) life.

Help! My Child Is Homeless

*I can do everything through Christ,
who gives me strength.*

PHILIPPIANS 4:13 NLT

Lord, I hurt so much. I need Your strength, and my adult child needs Your protection. We both need Your wisdom and guidance. (Name) has once again hit bottom, but this time, no one is left to come to the rescue. Not even me. This time (name's) addiction choices have taken everything but his (her) life.

(Name) has lost everything—his (her) car, apartment, license, self-respect, and dignity. He (she) has lied to and stolen from everyone who has tried to help. He (she) has abused countless public assistance programs. There are no more rehabs, shelters, or emergency vouchers available. No more loopholes. No one left to listen to the excuses, lies, and empty promises of an addict unwilling to admit that he (she) is powerless against the demons of alcohol and drugs.

No one except You.

I'm so broken, Lord, I don't know what to pray for anymore. There are no tears left to be cried. All I can say today is that I completely yield my adult child—and my heart—to Your care.

A Refreshing Hope

May the God who gives hope fill you with great joy.
May you have perfect peace as you trust in him. May
the power of the Holy Spirit fill you with hope.

ROMANS 15:13 NIRV

Dear Father, thank You for the power of the Holy Spirit. I praise Your name, for You invite us to Your throne to find hope through Your mercy and grace.

Lord, my adult child could use an extra portion of hope today as he (she) prepares to take important exams at school. (Name) has worked hard to get to this point. I'm confident that he (she) has worked hard to ensure a successful outcome. Please instill the same confidence in him (her).

By the power of the Holy Spirit, help (name) to sleep peacefully the night before these tests. Let (name) greet the morning feeling refreshed and full of joy, peace that passes all understanding, and hope that You have everything under control. Thank You, Lord, that our hope is in You alone.

Jesus, being (name's) parent has been a great honor and joy. Thank You for blessing me by sharing Your child with me.

A Clear Mind and Open Heart

*Praise be to the God and Father of our Lord
Jesus Christ! In his great mercy he has given
us new birth into a living hope through the
resurrection of Jesus Christ from the dead.*

1 PETER 1:3

Lord, we're surrounded by pain and suffering. We're confronted with news of violence, hunger, disease, or natural disasters every time we turn on the TV or computer. The information overload is wearing on us in countless ways—especially on our young people. Lord, please help us protect their hearts and minds today. May Your Holy Spirit convince them that hope is alive, faith is alive, and without a question, You are alive!

Father God, I pray You would also give my adult child a clear mind and an open heart to believe and trust in You, Your ways, and Your Word. Fill (name) with Your Spirit so he (she) may walk in wisdom and discernment. Give him (her) a sense of purpose and hope that enables him (her) to experience the life of Jesus every day.

Hold On

The eyes of the LORD are on those who fear him,
on those whose hope is in his unfailing love.

PSALM 33:18

"It's better to shake your fist at God than to turn your back on Him" (Max Lucado).

God, please show me how I can encourage my adult child to share his anger with You instead of turning a cold shoulder of disbelief and heartache. Fill my adult child with hope through the Holy Spirit. Show (name) that Your power and love can set him (her) free from the tyranny of disbelief and hopelessness.

Please, Lord, direct my steps and enlighten me with Your Spirit so I can help bring Your light into (name's) suffocating darkness. Lord, please, help me share HOPE (Hold On, Pain Ends) with my child. Give (name) strength to hold on during this painful season. Empower him (her) with the knowledge that this storm will end. Touch (name's) spirit with Your tender mercy.

I can no longer cradle my precious child in my arms and kiss away his (her) wounds. But You can, God. You can give (name) hope.

I—IMPLEMENT a Plan of Action

The "I" Step in SANITY

Dear children, let us not love with words or
speech but with actions and in truth.

1 John 3:18

Thank You, Lord, for showing me the need to apply the "I" step in SANITY and IMPLEMENT a plan of action. Help me follow through and set healthy boundaries to improve the quality of my life and the lives of those closest to me.

Father, the time has come for me to stop talking about how my adult child needs to change. I need to take action and make changes in my own life. Give me strength to stop enabling (name) and to detach from the drama he (she) brings to my life. Help me release everyone else's problems from my heart so I can finally see with new eyes the areas I need to change according to Your will. Help me conform my character to Christ's and reflect God's heart in my relationships with those I love.

Lord, grant me strength and peace so I can hear Your voice. Help me define healthy boundaries and implement a plan based on wisdom from Your Word.

Write the Vision

The LORD gave me this answer: "Write down clearly on tablets what I reveal to you, so that it can be read at a glance. Put it in writing, because it is not yet time for it to come true."

HABAKKUK 2:2-3 GNT

Lord, You developed an action plan long ago for all Your children, complete with commandments, blessings, promises, and prayers. You clearly defined right and wrong and gave firm yet loving consequences for disobedience. Your action plan is written with abundant grace, mercy, forgiveness, and love.

There's a saying that if we aim for nothing, we will hit it every time. Lord, I don't want to be aimless. I want to be obedient to You, hear Your Word, and see You at work in and around my life. Father, I want to experience Your presence and power in life-changing ways.

God, please help me outline a written plan that will identify where I'm going and what I need to do in order to get there. Help me discern habits to break, changes to make, and specific steps I can take to find my purpose in You.

They Will Be Comforted

Blessed are those who mourn,
for they will be comforted.

Matthew 5:4

Lord, it breaks my heart to think of (name) being in prison. He (she) faces locks, bars, and the threat of violence every day. Lord, please help me balance mercy and justice as (name) is held accountable for his (her) actions.

Father, You know how much I love my son (daughter). Please help me convey that love in a kind, positive, and spiritually empowering way. Direct our phone calls, letters, and visits, and use them to build bridges during this difficult time. Keep the enemy from inflating our disagreements or driving a wedge between us.

Give me strength not to be emotionally manipulated by (name's) attitude about this situation. Help both of us to focus not on the nightmare he (she) is enduring but on the steps he (she) needs to take to be released as soon as possible.

Lord, I ask in Jesus's name that (name) will connect with Christian inmates who are growing in their faith. Give my son (daughter) a desire to close the gap between himself (herself) and You through the power of the Holy Spirit and Your Word.

No More Hiding

He brought them out of darkness, the utter darkness,
and broke away their chains.

PSALM 107:14

Lord, I come to You with a heavy heart. My adult child has reached rock bottom from making so many wrong choices and is in prison today. Yet as devastating as this is, I know that You have a plan and that my son (daughter) is exactly where he (she) is supposed to be. No more running, no more hiding. I pray that (name) will use this time to reflect on the choices he (she) has made and will see that this isn't the life he (she) wants or that You intend him (her) to have.

Father, my deepest prayer is that inside those prison walls, my adult child will find a newfound freedom by entering into Your presence. That (name's) spirit will be set free as he (she) is comforted, delivered from sin, filled with hope and peace, and completely changed by Your all-consuming love, which You pour out on those who truly seek You.

God Will Fill You with Joy

May the God of hope fill you with all joy and
peace as you trust in him, so that you may overflow
with hope by the power of the Holy Spirit.

ROMANS 15:13

Lord, I thank You that the joy of the Lord is my strength. Father, I want to remember to pray the word "joy" in my time of prayer. The letter "J" reminds me to first praise *Jesus* for saving me and being the Lord of my life. The "O" is a great reminder to pray for *others*. What a privilege it is to stand in the gap for my friends, co-workers, colleagues, church family, and loved ones. Please never let me take this for granted. And lastly, God, the "Y" stands for *You*. As I bring my prayers, petitions, and praise to You at the foot of the cross, I thank You for giving Your life for me, for being but a breath-prayer away, always accessible, always on call.

Thank You, Lord, for Your promise to fill me with peace and JOY as I trust in You.

Joy

My Heart Is Yours

I have seen you in the sanctuary and beheld your power and your glory. Because your love is better than life, my lips will glorify you. I will praise you as long as I live, and in your name I will lift up my hands.

PSALM 63:2-4

Lord, You are mighty and powerful. I honor You with all of my being. With a word, You created this world. And with Your love, compassion, mercy, and grace, You gave Your Son on the cross for me. My heart is full of joy and peace when I look at all You've created. Thank You for opening the eyes of my heart to see You in the bud of a flower, the giggle of a small child, the beautiful clouds in the sky, and the sound of the rain.

I treasure Your love for me and long to share it with everyone—particularly with my adult child, who is having a difficult time right now seeing any joy in the world. I lift up (name) to You—praying that she (he) will one day be able to behold Your glory and majesty in the same refreshing way.

Free from the Law

*Therefore, there is now no condemnation for
those who are in Christ Jesus, because through
Christ Jesus the law of the Spirit who gives life
has set you free from the law of sin and death.*

ROMANS 8:1-2

Our legal system frightens me, Lord. My adult child is
navigating a convoluted labyrinth of legalities in a painful season of litigation.

Jesus, he (she) has so many papers to fill out, hoops
to jump through, and fees to pay—it's overwhelming.
Lord, please send godly professionals into (name's) life
who not only know and understand worldly law but
also love the spiritual law in Your holy Word.

Fill (name) with compassion and composure and
empower him (her) to behave with all parties involved
in a way that clearly demonstrates Your love flowing
through him (her). Jesus, when frustration and fear
threaten to overwhelm (name), fill him (her) with a
supernatural peace that passes all understanding. Give
(name) the assurance that You always care for those
who trust in You.

Grounded in You

My flesh and my heart may fail,
but God is the Rock and firm Strength of my heart
and my Portion forever.

PSALM 73:26 AMP

Lord, help me to follow Your Spirit and not be led by my emotions. When I base my decisions on how I feel from one moment to the next, I know I'm straying from the path You've set before me—especially in my relationship with (name). My heart can get so wrapped up in his (her) circumstances that my head can't think clearly. I end up responding to (name) in ways that handicap more than they help. Please help me to let go.

When I am grounded in You and Your Word, I can apply the "S" step in SANITY and STOP when I find myself getting emotionally caught up in the drama of (name's) life. When I remember to ask myself, "What's really going on here, and what would Jesus do?" I can stop responding emotionally and start responding rationally—with firmness and love.

Thank You for my newfound sanity. As I become more spiritually balanced, may (name) see more and more of You in me.

Do Not Fear Bad News

They do not fear bad news;
they confidently trust the LORD to care for them.

PSALM 112:7 NLT

Lord, I'm clinging to You as I'm releasing my adult child. But Father, I am weak. This is so difficult for me—please fill me with Your strength. For so long I've tried to "fix" people, but I've actually been enabling them and delaying the work You were doing through the Holy Spirit. Thank You for revealing this to me, helping me to repent, and forgiving me. Please continue teaching me to respond to people and problems in healthier ways.

Father, I know that Your timing is best and that You are often accomplishing more than I can see. I'm holding fast to the "T" step in SANITY as I TRUST the voice of the Spirit, who has convicted me to let go of (name) and let You do a good work in his (her) life. I love my adult child and will continue to pray without ceasing, but I will not swoop in and rescue him (her) from the consequences of his (her) choices. Instead, I trust You to be his (her) Comforter and Teacher.

Listening

A Teaching Moment

The Lord confides in those who fear him;
he makes his covenant known to them.

Psalm 25:14

Father God, today I found some spoiled food in the refrigerator. As I was throwing it away, I thought of some rotten things in my life.

I've made some poor choices, and I've used my energy in unhelpful ways. I've ignored these bad habits far too long, and as a result, my life has started to decay. I've been weary and burdened with negative feelings of guilt, anger, shame, fear, and unforgiveness. Now I see that these will continue to grow like mold until I get to the source of the problem.

Thank You for reminding me to clean out the refrigerator of my heart. I repent, Lord—I am throwing out the old, stale ways of relating—and I trust You to make my life fresh and clean again.

Pay Attention

My child, pay attention to what I say.
Listen carefully to my words.
Don't lose sight of them.
Let them penetrate deep into your heart,
for they bring life to those who find them,
and healing to their whole body.

PROVERBS 4:20-22 NLT

Father, I pray for better understanding of Your Word. Help me listen carefully to Your words, take them to heart, and obey them. I pray that each day, I won't look into another person's face until I've first looked into Your face through Your Word. I know, Lord, this is where I will receive healing for my body, soul, and spirit.

Today, I especially pray You would heal my broken heart. Please help me not look in the rearview mirror of my life, but look forward to the mighty work You're doing in me and in my prodigal children. Help us to walk forward in faith, knowing You have every detail of our lives in the palm of Your hand.

Lord, I am paying attention to what You say, and I thank You this day and always for Your healing power.

Thoughts of the Heart

I will give you a new heart and a new mind.
I will take away your stubborn heart of stone
and give you an obedient heart.

EZEKIEL 36:26 GNT

Lord, You've blessed me with many happy childhood memories, and they continue to shape my life in positive ways. However, I also have some unhappy memories, and for a long time, I was consumed by them. They too shaped my behavior. Thank You for healing my heart and teaching me how to deal with negative memories so they no longer control my life!

I pray You will show my adult child how to experience this as well. Deeply traumatic experiences have had a lasting impact on (name). God, I ask You to restore good memories to his (her) mind and help him (her) celebrate the positive things You have done. Teach him (her) how to handle the bad memories, laying them at Your feet. May their power diminish and eventually disappear. Lord, please heal the little boy (girl) that still lives deep inside the heart of my adult child.

Stop the Flow of Money

Behold, I will bring to it health and healing,
and I will heal them and reveal to them
abundance of prosperity and security.
JEREMIAH 33:6 ESV

Dear Lord, my adult child is in financial trouble again. Should I help? If I don't help, what will happen? Father, help me not to jump to a conclusion too quickly. You know I have a tendency to take things into my own hands. That hasn't worked well so far.

Lord, is now the time to call out the "S" step in SANITY and STOP the flow of money? Help me also implement the "A" step and ASSEMBLE supportive people who will give me objective feedback. I confess I'm not objective about this situation at all. I know I shouldn't open my checkbook time and again, but I can't seem to break this habit and get off the gerbil wheel of insanity.

Lord, please give me the strength to make the right choice for (name)—a choice that will lead him (her) to accept responsibility for his (her) own financial choices.

The Currency of the Heart

May God, who gives this patience and encouragement,
help you live in complete harmony with each
other, as is fitting for followers of Christ Jesus.

ROMANS 15:5 NLT

God, in this fast and furious life, I've become too busy, too hurried, and too self-centered to live in harmony with those I love. I've settled for quick fixes and haven't patiently cooperated with Your plan. Somewhere along the way, simply writing a check to get my daughter (son) out of trouble became easier than stopping long enough to consider what was best for her (him). I'm sorry, Lord.

I've complained that (name) is selfish and comes around only when she (he) wants something—usually money. The sad truth is, I've often enabled this behavior by taking the quick and easy way out. But love isn't measured in dollar signs, and although I've been financially generous, I've been stingy with the currency of my heart, time, and prayers.

Forgive me, Jesus. Help me apply the "S" step in SANITY and STOP the crazy pace, STOP the flow of money, and STOP living on the gerbil wheel of insanity.

The "N" Step in SANITY

Blessed is the one whom God corrects;
so do not despise the discipline of the Almighty.
For he wounds, but he also binds up;
he injures, but his hands also heal.

JOB 5:17-18

Heavenly Father, I ask for strength as I resolve to stop giving in to my adult child's excuses, lies, and manipulation. Open my eyes to see the truth more clearly. Help me respond to (name) with newfound firmness and love in situations that once caused weakness and fear. I will no longer accept or make excuses for unacceptable and wrong behavior. I will no longer allow myself to get caught up in the chaos of (name's) life.

I confess that sometimes I feel too weak to stop this negative pattern of excusing his (her) behavior. I need Your strength and power in my life today so I can continue standing strong. Thank You, Lord, for reminding me of the corrections I need to make in my own life in order to walk in alignment with You. Help (name) understand that I'm making new choices and new responses because I love him (her).

A Rude Awakening

Blessed is the one who trusts in the LORD,
whose confidence is in him.

JEREMIAH 17:7

Lord, I want to grow, to live a full life—and I want my adult child to do the same. For this to happen, some things must change, beginning with me. It's time for me to own up to my own responsibility and stop making excuses for my adult child's unacceptable behavior and poor choices.

I had a rude awakening when I began listing all the excuses (name) and I have made. The list is long. I should have nipped many of these excuses in the bud a long time ago. However, I'm thankful the scales have fallen from my eyes. Thank You, Jesus, for showing me the part I've played in my challenging relationship with my adult child.

God, help me be the kind of firm and loving parent You want me to be. Help me stay strong and keep my eyes focused on You. Lord, show me how to jump off the gerbil wheel of insanity and find sanity in Your loving arms. My hope, trust, and confidence are in You.

Reorganizing Relationships

My God will meet all your needs
according to the riches of his glory in Christ Jesus.

PHILIPPIANS 4:19

Heavenly Father, my adult child and I have a strained relationship. We have weak emotional boundaries, so I'm often controlled by his (her) feelings. With all the drama, sometimes I feel as if I'm caught in a hurricane with no protection.

Father, please help me show compassion, mercy, and love but also demonstrate healthy boundaries and balanced living. I can't do this on my own—I need Your help to make important changes. Help me follow Your Spirit and obey Your Word so can I receive a new nature. Show me how to reorganize my relationships by putting You first and accepting my responsibilities in Christ. As I prioritize daily time with You, reading Your Word, praying, praising, and worshipping, I trust that I will become more like Christ.

And I trust that I will begin to find hope and healing in my relationship with my adult child.

Put What You Learn into Practice

Whatever you have learned or received or heard
from me, or seen in me—put it into practice.
And the God of peace will be with you.

PHILIPPIANS 4:9

Lord, I prayed for wisdom and discernment, and You showed me that I must apply the "S" step in SANITY and STOP trying to fix things that only You can fix.

I want to be an obedient child, Father, and to put into practice the things You're teaching me. Please help me let go of the things I cannot control and instead focus on what You would have me do. Give me spiritual ears to hear Your voice and receive Your divine direction. Give me Your strength to make good choices, and lead me to the wisdom of Your Word. I'm taking the "Y" step in SANITY and YIELDING control to You.

As I confidently follow You one step and one day at a time, I pray that You will bless me and my family. Empower me to be the example You have asked me to be.

Independence Day

I will refresh the weary and satisfy the faint.

JEREMIAH 31:25

Lord, I've heard it said, "You can't paddle another man's canoe for him." God, I confess that I've been paddling my adult child's canoe far too long. Now (name) must learn how to paddle his (her) own canoe.

Please show me what (name) is actually capable of. Is he (she) able to pilot his (her) own boat? Years ago (name) started using drugs and alcohol to escape life, and now many of (name's) social and emotional skills are stunted. Lord, help me to have reasonable expectations.

Please lead us to an experienced professional who can properly evaluate (name's) skills. Give me the strength and wisdom to stop numbing his (her) pain and enabling his (her) unhealthy dependence on me. Help me change my own distorted views and character defects so I can help (name) become the emotionally whole adult You want him (her) to be. Show me how to respond to (name's) choices in ways that will encourage and empower (name) to become as independent as possible. I choose to cooperate with You one day at a time.

This Time…

All the people saw him walking and
heard him praising God.

ACTS 3:9 NLT

Dear Jesus, my adult child is once again in recovery for his (her) addiction. You know how hard this is for me to watch. I've been through it before and hoped I wouldn't have to go through it again. But here it is. And so I ask You, Lord, for strength to lay (name) entirely at Your feet and trust for a good outcome.

Lord, this time I'd like to see a miracle. This time I'd like to see (name) admit his (her) powerlessness over this addiction. This time I'd like to see (name) take complete responsibility for his (her) recovery. This time I'd like to see (name) develop a growing desire to do the right thing in all things. This time, I'd like to see a light in (name's) eyes and a hope in his (her) heart. Gracious God, I praise Your name for this coming miraculous gift.

Father, please empower me to see this by faith and in reality—one step at a time, one day at a time.

Approaching You in Confidence

This is the confidence we have in approaching God:
that if we ask anything according to his will, he hears
us. And if we know that he hears us—whatever we
ask—we know that we have what we asked of him.

1 John 5:14-15

God, thank You for the opportunity to enjoy conversations with You—opportunities to show You my love and build my relationship with You. I confess that sometimes I come to You only when I'm in desperate need. How arrogant—how shallow!

Heavenly Father, Your still, small voice calms my soul. You love me with an everlasting love and have drawn me with loving-kindness. The longer I stay in Your presence and the more I grow in Your Word, the deeper my love, trust, and confidence become.

Please help me, God, to pray according to Your will—in a way that brings You glory, honor, and praise. Your Word assures me that I can pray for anything, and if I have faith, I will receive it. Help me call out in confidence to You on behalf of those I love.

Prayer

The Lord Will Raise Them Up

*The prayer offered in faith will make the sick
person well; the Lord will raise them up. If
they have sinned, they will be forgiven.*

JAMES 5:15

Lord, I thank You every day for what You're doing in
the life of my adult child. As Your divine power works
through (name), may he (she) learn to depend on You
more and more. May he (she) come to know the comfort of the Almighty God, who forgives all sin and loves
beyond all measure.

Help (name) know that You are faithful, merciful,
gracious, and wise. Open the eyes of (name's) heart to
seek You not only in times of trial and tribulation, but
at all times. God, please give (name) an unshakable
faith in You and a hunger deep within to walk in Your
will, power, and purpose.

Breathe new life into (name's) spirit today. Give
him (her) a desire to communicate with You through
intentional prayer. Reveal the truth of Your forgiveness
and the power of Your love. Guide (name) to seek the
living water of Your Word in refreshing moments of
heartfelt communication with You.

Tell God What You Need

Don't worry about anything; instead, pray
about everything. Tell God what you need,
and thank him for all he has done.

PHILIPPIANS 4:6 NLT

Father God, I humble myself before You and thank You
for the power of prayer. In Jesus's name, I commit to
living free of worry and anxiety. I praise You for fulfill-
ing Your purpose for my loved ones and me. I focus
my thoughts and actions on what is true, honest, just,
pure, lovely, and of good report. Today, I'm going to set
aside the sin of worry. I'm so thankful that I don't have
to worry about anything, but by prayer and supplica-
tion, with thanksgiving, I can present my requests to
You, trusting that Your peace, which passes all understanding, will guard my heart and mind.

Thank You for this awesome promise. I praise Your
holy name!

Push Through the Pain

Wait patiently for the LORD.
Be brave and courageous.
Yes, wait patiently for the LORD.

PSALM 27:14 NLT

Lord, how long am I supposed to pray for my adult child's eyes to be opened? For his (her) heart of stone to be replaced with a heart of flesh? I've been holding the rope for my loved one for such a long time—I'm not sure how much longer I can hang on. My faith in You stays strong, Lord, but I've grown weary. Will I ever see changes occur in (name's) life?

God, help me to PUSH (Pray Until Something Happens) through the pain and weariness. Show me how to pray effectively for (name), and strengthen me with Your Spirit so I will persevere and not give up. I choose to trust that Your timing is perfect. I believe that regardless of whether I hear Your voice, You are working. I claim Your promise that "the prayer of a righteous person is powerful and effective" (James 5:16).

Lord, You are an on-time God. Please give me the patience to wait on You as I continue to pray intentionally and fervently for (name).

Great and Precious Gifts

He has given us the very great and precious gifts
he promised, so that by means of these gifts you
may escape from the destructive lust that is in the
world, and may come to share the divine nature.

2 PETER 1:4 GNT

God, You have given me some awesome promises in
Your Word. I'm thankful today that I'm a new creation
in Christ and that You are making me more and more
like You. I pray that my zest for life, which flows from a
deep understanding and appreciation of Your promises,
will flow over into the lives of those I love.

Thank You for Your promise that we're never alone
during any trial. That You will empower us to endure
the most difficult circumstances. That we will receive
anything if we ask in Your name. That You will renew
our strength when we hope in You. That absolutely
nothing can separate us from Your love.

Father, give my loved ones abundant faith to believe
that all things are possible in Your will.

God's Pleasure and Purpose

*God had already decided that through Jesus
Christ he would make us his children—
this was his pleasure and purpose.*

EPHESIANS 1:5 GNT

Lord, sometimes my adult child feels lost and aimless and without a true sense of purpose. But (name's) existence is not an accident. You had a plan and purpose for (name) before she (he) was even born. Please help (name) believe and claim this truth. Please open (name's) eyes and heart to see the life You have in mind for her (him). Remind (name) of the gifts You have given her (him). Help her (him) see that there is more to life than just the here and now—that Your purpose for her (him) will last for eternity.

Give my beloved daughter (son) the discernment to apply the "T" step in SANITY and TRUST the still, small voice of the Spirit as she (he) prays for wisdom to walk in Your will. Thank You for the Holy Spirit, who teaches us how to live.

He Has His Eye on Us

*It's in Christ that we find out who we are and what
we are living for. Long before we first heard of Christ
and got our hopes up, he had his eye on us, had
designs on us for glorious living, part of the overall
purpose he is working out in everything and everyone.*

EPHESIANS 1:11 MSG

Lord, thank You for bringing a sense of purpose back into my life. Before I was (name's) parent, I was Your child—fearfully and wonderfully made for a divine purpose.

In my early parenting days, I was certain my purpose was to protect my child from danger, shield him (her) from the harsh realities of life, and provide a way of life I never had. As (name) grew, so did my sense of responsibility. Eventually I became consumed with trying to fix and rescue (name) from the consequences of poor choices. I thought I was helping, but I was getting in Your way. And somewhere along the way, I lost sight of my own identity.

Lord, help me be the person You created me to be and a blessing to the people around me.

Knock Down Strongholds

*It is true that I am an ordinary, weak human being,
but I don't use human plans and methods to win
my battles. I use God's mighty weapons, not those
made by men, to knock down the devil's strongholds.*

2 Corinthians 10:3-4 TLB

Father, thank You for the power of praise, which paralyzes the enemy. May my words and actions honor You today. Thank You for the armor of God, with which I can stand against the wiles of the devil. Thank You for removing anxiety as I present my requests to You in prayer. Thank You for giving me the mind of Christ.

Father, You say that I can bind on earth what You have bound in heaven, and I can loose on earth what You have loosed in heaven. Thank You for destroying works of the devil, for making a public spectacle of him by the cross. Thank You for making us more than conquerors in all our struggles. Thank You for never allowing anything to separate us from Your love. Thank You, Lord, for victory.

Rebuke the Enemy

Get Away, Satan

*While the boy was coming, the demon threw
him to the ground in a convulsion. But
Jesus rebuked the impure spirit, healed the
boy and gave him back to his father.*

LUKE 9:42

Lord, thank You for protecting my adult child from
the enemy. Thank You for covering him (her) with
the blood of Jesus and putting a hedge of protection
around him (her). Be his (her) refuge from any evil
influences that would threaten him (her).

Lord, please help my son (daughter) never to give
the devil a foothold in his (her) life. Heavenly Father, I
pray that You would reveal any greed, pride, covetous-
ness, slander, lying, manipulating, shame, guilt, or sexual sin so that (name) may recognize it, repent of it, and
turn it over to You. Help him (her) to close all those
doors of enemy access.

As You renew (name's) mind through the power of
the Spirit, keep him (her) free from any deceptive sug-
gestions and thoughts the enemy would use to corrupt
and destroy. Give (name) the wisdom, discernment,
and supernatural strength to live in Your will and be set
free from the traps and bondages of Satan.

Rebuke the Enemy

I Will Not Revert

The Lord is faithful, and he will strengthen
you and protect you from the evil one.

2 THESSALONIANS 3:3

Lord, at one time, my family and I barely registered as a blip on Satan's radar. The enemy didn't need to waste his energy on us once he'd poisoned us with his lies. Damaged and dysfunctional, without faith or hope, we were of little concern to Satan and no threat to his plan for mass destruction. But when our family began the search for freedom, we seemed to meet resistance at every turn.

Father, I pray for protection over my entire family as we stand against the evil around us. May the Spirit of Christ fill every nook and cranny of our lives. Let Your light pierce the darkness around us. Let Your truth replace any lies we may be tempted to believe. We will not turn back, but will press on toward Your wonderful plan for us. In the name of the Father, Son, and Holy Spirit, we declare that the enemy has no place here.

Relationships

Patience with One Another

*Bear with each other and forgive one
another if any of you has a grievance against
someone. Forgive as the Lord forgave you.*

Colossians 3:13

Father, thank You for my adult child and his (her) spouse. Thank You for creating both of them with unique gifts and talents. I pray that they would use their gifts to build each other up and not to tear each other down.

Lord, bless their relationship. Strengthen the bond between them and give them a strong sense of love and respect for each other. Help them look to You for salvation, wisdom, and guidance. Please bring them closer together as they draw closer to You. God, protect them from bitterness and anger. Let patience and kindness permeate their home so they can live in joy and peace.

Forgive me for the times I've gotten in the middle of their disputes. I relinquish my desire to fix things, and instead I give my adult child and his (her) spouse to You. Heal their past hurts and help them move forward with strength together. May they enjoy a happy, healthy home that reflects Your wonderful love for us.

God Is Extraordinarily Patient

The Lord isn't really being slow about his
promise, as some people think. No, he is being
patient for your sake. He does not want anyone
to be destroyed, but wants everyone to repent.

2 PETER 3:9 NLT

Father God, as a Christian, I ache when my adult child embraces a worldly tolerance to sin. As a parent, I feel as if my heart is breaking. I never expected (name) to turn away from his (her) spiritual roots and pursue such destructive influences. This isn't the same person who grew up in our house. He (she) has changed so much because of the world's attractions.

God, an inner battle is waging in (name)—thank You for prompting change! I know that (name) doesn't really want the life he (she) is creating. I believe he (she) knows deep within that he (she) is on the wrong path. This selfish pursuit of satisfaction is out of alignment with Your will and inhibits the growth of the fruit of the Spirit—love, joy, peace, patience, kindness, goodness, faithfulness, gentleness, and self-control.

Merciful Lord, please give (name) wisdom and courage to change direction and do the right thing.

Choosing You

*There will be more rejoicing in heaven over
one sinner who repents than over ninety-nine
righteous persons who do not need to repent.*

LUKE 15:7

I was blind but now I see! Lord, thank You for show-ing me the person I was becoming. As I focused on my adult child's need to repent, I neglected my own call to repentance. I wasn't walking the talk, and I'm so sorry. Forgive me for trying to fix others and change things I had no power to change. Trying to remove the twigs in other people's eyes, I neglected the plank in my own.

Thank You for the healing and other blessings I have received from truly repenting. I was waiting for You to change the difficult people in my life, but You were eagerly waiting for me to acknowledge my own need to change. You nudged my heart to repent and changed me from the inside out. Anxiety, doubt, and fear are gone—peace, security, and joy have come!

Thank You for revealing Your perfect will to my heart through Your Spirit. Heaven is rejoicing today because of the grace, mercy, and love You have shown me.

Responsibility

Bring Your Own Shovel

Pay careful attention to your own work, for then
you will get the satisfaction of a job well done, and
you won't need to compare yourself to anyone else.
For we are each responsible for our own conduct.

GALATIANS 6:4-5 NLT

God, I know I shouldn't accept responsibility for other people's bad choices. As I learn to set healthy boundaries with my adult children, please show me what is my responsibility and what is not. I confess that my heart and mind are often at odds.

I've heard it said that You will move mountains on our behalf, but You still want us to show up and bring a shovel. You will work miracles in our lives, but we must do our part and cooperate with You. Lord, help me to stop taking the shovel from my adult child's hand. Please give him (her) the strength and will to pick it up on his (her) own and dig his (her) way out of the pit of poor choices and uncomfortable consequences. Please help (name) and me carry out our own responsibilities in ways that bring You glory.

The "S" Step in SANITY

"The time has come," he said. "The kingdom of God has come near. Repent and believe the good news!"

MARK 1:15

Father God, I'm ready to stop negative behaviors that have kept me from being the parent and the person You want me to be. I don't want to remain on the gerbil wheel of insanity, repeating the same actions and expecting different results.

Lord, thank You for showing me that I cannot change the choices others make (especially my adult child's), but I can change my responses to them. You have made it clear that sanity will begin only when I repent of wrong choices I've made and learn to make new choices aligned with Your Word and will. God, help me apply this first step in SANITY in all my relationships. As I apply the "S" step and STOP the things that keep me from growing closer to You, I know I will grow closer to others in authentic and God-honoring ways.

Lord, help me stop going backward and start moving forward with You.

Guard Your Heart

Above all else, guard your heart,
for everything you do flows from it.

PROVERBS 4:23

Dear Lord, sometimes I want to scream, "Stop the world; I want to get off!" I feel as if life is moving too fast and I can't keep up. Please help me get off the gerbil wheel of insanity and obey Your command to the psalmist—"Be still, and know that I am God." Quiet my heart and help me learn from You.

God, show me my negative behaviors that are hurting my relationships, particularly with my adult child. Empower me to exercise God-honoring control of my life so I can guard my heart and fulfill Your destiny for me. I reject excuses and the lies of the enemy. Give me the wisdom and discernment to stop, step back, and be still. Fill me with the wisdom of Your Word, and help me to replace negative self-talk with positive words that manifest Your Spirit flowing through me.

Soften Her Heart

*God so loved the world that he gave his one
and only Son, that whoever believes in him
shall not perish but have eternal life.*

Lord, I come humbly to You today and ask that You soften my adult child's heart so she (he) can know Your grace, mercy, and unconditional love. My precious daughter (son) is empty and needs to be filled. She (he) is stuck in confusion, pain, and hopelessness because she (he) can't fill the emptiness.

In Your holy name, Lord, I ask You to show (name) that You alone are the answer. Only You can bring true satisfaction. I ask that You draw (name) to Your heart through the Spirit of truth and show her (him) Your magnificent love and forgiveness in tangible ways.

Help (name) not to be ruled by her (his) emotions—especially anger, jealousy, and hatred. Empower (name) to let go of destructive choices and to surrender her (his) emptiness to You. You will fill her (him) with a peace that passes all understanding and bring us everlasting freedom.

Renewed like Eagles

Praise the LORD, my soul; all my inmost being,
praise his holy name. Praise the LORD, my soul, and
forget not all his benefits—who forgives all your
sins and heals all your diseases, who redeems your
life from the pit and crowns you with love and
compassion, who satisfies your desires with good
things so that your youth is renewed like the eagle's.

PSALM 103:1-5

Lord, thank You for Your redeeming love and compassion—especially now. My adult child is struggling, and the situation has gone from bad to worse. Yet I know that Your love never fails and Your plan is sovereign. I know that by grace and through faith my son (daughter) can and will be saved.

Father, I believe in Your miraculous power to lift lost souls out of the pit of despair. I pray that as (name) hits rock bottom, he (she) will reach up, cry out to You, and find Your supernatural strength. God, give (name) a repentant and open heart. May he (she) let go of guilt and shame and know without question that You have already extended forgiveness. Thank You for loving him (her) with an unfailing love.

Bringing Fear out of Darkness

*Like a city whose walls are broken through
is a person who lacks self-control.*

PROVERBS 25:28

God, my adult child is emotionally unstable. I'm afraid because I don't know what's going to happen to him (her). Please give me a wise and discerning spirit as I pray, and guide me to helpful information and resources.

Lord, (name's) disregard for social norms, impulsive behavior, and indifference to the rights and feelings of others all seem to fit the description of antisocial personality disorder. He (she) doesn't make plans, ignores obligations, and can't follow the law. He (she) is reckless and underhanded, shows no remorse, and often has a bad temper. Something is seriously wrong with his (her) conscience.

Father, (name) needs help with this psychological disorder. Please show me what to do. I pray for wisdom and strength to do the right thing. I know (name) is not beyond my prayers or Your restoration, God. You can work in miraculous ways to bring Your children out of bondage and into freedom and peace. I ask for Your divine will to be done in my son (daughter)—and in all things.

Sacred Intimacy

Let the Holy Spirit guide your lives. Then you won't be doing what your sinful nature craves.

GALATIANS 5:16 NLT

God, I pray that You would help my adult child to be sexually responsible. (Name) has been involved in many short-term intimate relationships, and some of them have yielded long-term consequences. Father, please show (name) that she (he) is looking for love in all the wrong places. Help her (him) to see the long-term emotional and spiritual damage that sexual misconduct causes. I believe in Your miraculous power to turn people around in their thoughts and actions, so I'm praying You will show (name) the need to be sexually responsible.

God, (name) longs to love and be loved. She (he) desires connection with another person. Please, Lord, fill her (his) heart with Your love, which alone can satisfy. May the love she (he) shares with other people be an overflow of Your great love for her (him).

Forgive me, Lord, for any part I have played in the continuation of this sinful behavior. I know I'm not responsible for the choices (name) is making, but I am responsible to bring everything to You in prayer.

The "T" Step in SANITY

*Whether you turn to the right or to the
left, your ears will hear a voice behind you,
saying, "This is the way; walk in it."*

ISAIAH 30:21

Father God, thank You for the gift of Your Holy
Spirit—the Spirit of truth. I'm so thankful I can lean
on You with all my heart, mind, and soul—even when
I don't understand. Thank You for Your still, small voice,
which heals my heart and transforms my life.

Jesus, help me to apply the "T" step in SANITY
and TRUST the voice of the Spirit. That will bring me
closer to You and help me understand Your will and
purpose for my life. May I hear Your voice clearly as
I seek the truth, especially regarding my relationship
with my adult child.

God, help me find strength to make wise choices.
Convict me of Your will for my life in all things. Give
me a discerning mind, a kind heart, and a teachable
spirit as I trust in You to tell me the way to walk and
then joyfully walk in it.

God Will Bring It to Pass

Take delight in the LORD,
and he will give you your heart's desires.
Commit everything you do to the LORD.
Trust him, and he will help you.

PSALM 37:4-5 NLT

Father God, sometimes the noise around me drowns out Your voice. Please show me how to stop that from happening. Help me to entrust my way to You so I can walk in Your will. I'm confident that as I trust in You and Your voice, my stress will decrease and my peace will increase. What a blessing!

Father, I pray my adult child will also trust Your voice. In the mighty name of Jesus and by the power of His blood, I commit (name) to Your loving care and direction. Help (name) trust You completely and grow closer to You. I pray You will enable her (him) to feel the peace that passes all understanding.

Father God, I trust You to bring everything to pass that You have promised in Your Word.

I Trust in You, Lord

I trust in you, LORD;
I say, "You are my God."
My times are in your hands.

PSALM 31:14-15

Father, You are sovereign. I worship You today. Your Word promises that in all things You work for the good of those who love You, who have been called according to Your purpose. Lord, I want to trust You without terms, knowing that You will go before me to prepare the way even when I get impatient and don't understand. My times are in Your hands. You have spoken to my heart that delay is not denial. Lord, I want to wait on You and trust You unconditionally. I trust You with my life and the lives of my loved ones, and I pray a special covering on the life of my adult child. God, please reveal Your love to (name).

Lord, I praise You and commit this day to You, for Your glory.

Thankfulness

No Greater Gift

There is surely a future hope for you,
and your hope will not be cut off.

PROVERBS 23:18

Lord God, I pray that nothing will ever separate (name) from Your powerful love and merciful compassion.

God, I know life isn't easy for young people today. The situations (name) faces daily are rife with the influence of a dark and dangerous enemy. Give (name) the wisdom and discernment to identify those influences. Give her (him) the power through the blood of Jesus to overcome any evil that would infiltrate her (his) heart. Lord, help (name) enjoy healthy relationships with people who build her (him) up. May she (he) live in Your grace, mercy, and forgiveness every day as she (he) walks with You.

Father, I will forever dream big dreams for (name) and wish her (him) all the blessings and happiness You can provide. May she (he) walk in right relationship with You with a joyful heart and a thankful spirit. Holy God, You can give no greater gift than a child who embraces Your name and longs to walk in Your will. Thank You for this precious gift. I will love You all my life.

My Pride Is in the Lord

It is we who are the circumcision, we who
serve God by his Spirit, who boast in Christ
Jesus, and who put no confidence in the flesh.

PHILIPPIANS 3:3

God, I am so proud—not of myself, but of You!

Father, I resist the sin of self-centered pride. I still have a long way to go, but I'm so thankful for the changes You're making in me. Continue to put a teachable spirit in me so I will boast only in You. Thank You for teaching me to move out of the way and let You do Your work in and through me.

When I walk in Your will and allow Your Spirit to flow through me, I find myself able to influence my family in ways I never dreamed possible. Thank You for the spiritual inheritance I'm able to give my children as a result of what You've given me. Thank You for helping me to show (name) what it means to walk humbly in the love, grace, and mercy of Christ.

I praise You today for filling me with pride—not in who I am, but in whose I am.

Spiritual Discipline

*Physical exercise has some value, but spiritual
exercise is valuable in every way, because it promises
life both for the present and for the future.*

1 TIMOTHY 4:8 GNT

Lord, a friend recently shared that before she gets out of bed in the morning she always says, "This is the day the Lord has made—I will rejoice and be glad in it." She developed this spiritual discipline over the years, and it helped to change her life. Thank You, Lord, for the blessings that come from exercising spiritual discipline.

Please motivate my son (daughter) to exercise spiritual discipline. I pray that (name) will develop a burning desire to learn everything possible about You. That his (her) relationship with You would become the most important thing in his (her) life. I pray for (name) to grasp the power of prayer and feel a healthy burden to pray for himself (herself) and those he (she) cares about.

In the name of Jesus, I believe all of this is possible. I believe that with Your power and love, (name) can develop a spiritual discipline that will profoundly change his (her) life.

Tough Love

Firm and Loving

Jesus looked straight at them and answered,
"This is impossible for human beings, but
for God everything is possible."
MATTHEW 19:26 GNT

God, can You please confirm that I'm responding to my adult child's choices correctly? I feel convinced that this current direction is not where You want me or my family to go, and I can no longer be an accomplice in (name's) destructive lifestyle. How can I exhibit tough love in a way that honors You and helps (name)?

God, please show me how to be firm and loving at the same time. Help me to consistently apply the SANITY Steps in challenging situations and circumstances so I may develop more effective God-honoring habits. Show me through Your wisdom and Your Word how I can respond in a godly way to the lifestyle choices (name) makes. Give me clarity and discernment to act rationally and not emotionally when I speak to (name). Help me convey in the right words and actions that I deeply love (name) but cannot condone his (her) sin.

Taking a Stand

He lifted me out of the slimy pit,
out of the mud and mire;
he set my feet on a rock
and gave me a firm place to stand.

PSALM 40:2

Father, in Jesus's name, I pray against denial and helplessness in (name's) life. I repent of my part in enabling him (her) to accept these depressing emotions. I wanted to help, but I allowed (name) to sustain destructive patterns and disrupt our family. I didn't hold (name) accountable, and the effect has been devastating. Lord, for all of this, I ask Your forgiveness.

With Your Word and the strength of the SANITY Steps to guide me, I'm prepared to take a stand and take back my life. I will no longer allow (name's) irresponsible choices to manipulate my heart or damage my family's health. Please empower me through the Holy Spirit to set new boundaries in a way that honors You and helps (name). Give me courage to face whatever consequences occur as a result. Guide my steps and watch over my mouth during this season of tough love. Thank You in advance for restoring peace to my heart and our household.

Truth

Set You Free

You will know the truth,
and the truth will set you free.
JOHN 8:32

Father, I praise You for helping me to know the truth. Thank You setting me free—releasing me from spiritual bondage and bringing healing refreshment to my soul.

Today, I pray that my adult child will find this miraculous freedom. Freedom from anger, hurt, and pain. Freedom from anxiety, depression, and addiction. Freedom from any stronghold that holds him (her) captive.

God, I also thank You for Your living and active Word, which never returns to You void. Thank You, Father, for hiding Your Word deep in our hearts, teaching us and empowering us to rise up out of our struggles and overcome our difficulties as You do a new work in our lives each day. As we know Your truth, we can be set free.

And I especially thank You for Your Son, who died on the cross to set us free and give us eternal life.

A Gift from God

God saved you by his grace when you believed.
And you can't take credit for this; it is a gift from
God. Salvation is not a reward for the good things
we have done, so none of us can boast about it.

Ephesians 2:8-9 nlt

God, please reveal the truth of Your love to my son
(daughter). Breathe Your mercy and grace into (name's)
life. Strip away the veil of Satan's lies and remove the
blinders of disobedient rebellion from (name's) eyes.
Please soften his (her) hard and bitter heart and help
my precious son (daughter) to know the truth that will
set him (her) free. Give (name) the spirit of wisdom and
revelation as he (she) turns from sinful ways and trusts
the miraculous power of Your love and forgiveness.

Lord, instill in (name) the knowledge that You are
far more interested in what You can do for him (her)
than in what he (she) can do for You. Let (name) know
that Your first desire is to show how much You love
him (her).

God's Favor

> *As God's co-workers we urge you not to receive*
> *God's grace in vain. For he says, "In the time*
> *of my favor I heard you, and in the day of*
> *salvation I helped you." I tell you, now is the*
> *time of God's favor, now is the day of salvation.*

2 CORINTHIANS 6:1-2

Lord, You tell us in Your Word that our salvation is based on Your favor, which is on all of us who believe. One touch of Your favor can change our lives forever. Amen!

I know You want us to live in victory, God. When the odds are against us, You are always for us. We cannot be defeated. As the CEO of heaven and earth, You have a successful strategic plan already in place for us.

Thank You, God, for the victories You have already given us and those still to come. Thank You for Your favor on our lives. Thank You for helping my adult child to persevere through all the problems he (she) is facing and emerge from them stronger than ever. Show (name) the reality of Your favor and love and what it means to live a truly victorious life.

Accept No Substitutes

If you say, "The LORD is my refuge," and you make the Most High your dwelling, no harm will overtake you, no disaster will come near your tent.

PSALM 91:9-10

"God, grant me the ability to accept the things I cannot change, the courage to change the things I can, and the wisdom to know the difference."

Thank You for sharing this wisdom with my adult child, Lord. Help her (him) to discern what she (he) should and should not accept. May she (he) not accept any of Satan's lies. May she (he) not accept the godless values of this world. May she (he) not accept a low opinion of her (his) value and potential.

Instead, may she (he) accept Your promise that You will keep us safe if we look to You as our protector. May she accept that You are a loving God and not vengeful. That You work in all things. That You are our light and our salvation, and that we have nothing to fear.

A Wonderful Promise

He changes times and seasons;
he deposes kings and raises up others.
He gives wisdom to the wise
and knowledge to the discerning.

DANIEL 2:21

Lord, You tell us in Your Word that if we ask for wisdom, You will give it to us liberally. You assure us that You will do immeasurably more than all we ask or imagine. I praise You, God, for these wonderful promises and blessings.

Father, I want to do the right thing—and to know clearly what that is. Today, I pray for wisdom and a discerning spirit for every decision I make. Show me how You want me to influence the spiritual and emotional welfare of my adult child in this season of life.

Lord, help me provide what (name) needs, not what I want. Speak in and through me by the power of the Holy Spirit. Speak Your love, divine discernment, and wisdom directly into (name's) heart. Open the eyes of (name's) heart and leave no room for doubt that You are the King of kings and the sovereign Creator of all that has gone before and all that will ever be.

Someone You're Not

A false witness will not go unpunished,
nor will a liar escape.

PROVERBS 19:5 NLT

Dear Lord, You created (name) in Your image with a plan and purpose for her (his) life. However, it's always been difficult for (name) to claim that unique identity and embrace Your unconditional acceptance. Instead, (name) has always tried to be accepted by her (his) peers. Sadly, this acceptance has had countless conditions and has led to self-destructive choices with dangerous consequences.

Lord, the older (name) gets, the more she (he) desires acceptance based on worldly standards. Please show (name) the danger of always needing to fit in. Open (name's) eyes to see Your intense love and complete acceptance—based on *whose* we are, not on *who* we are, and certainly not on what kind of car we drive, where we buy our clothes, or how often we can pick up the tab.

Father, I continue to entrust (name) to Your care, guidance, and discipline. Please help me respond to her (his) choices in ways that honor You and help her (him) to be the person You're calling her (him) to be.

All God's Children

You are all children of God
through faith in Christ Jesus.
GALATIANS 3:26 NLT

Heavenly Father, in a world of uncertainty and never-ending change, I'm so thankful for Your consistent love for me. Thank You for using the trials and tribulations in my life to help me be more like You. Thank You for hope and healing and for restoring my life. I know You can do the same for my adult child.

Lord, it's never too late for You to restore (name's) life. You're always at work—even if I can't always see the progress. Thank You for leading me to this message of SANITY and for the insight I'm gaining as I apply the six steps to all my situations, circumstances, and relationships—especially the tenuous one with my adult child.

I know my life is built on a solid rock that can never be moved. I pray for opportunities to share the truth of Your love—and of SANITY—with others. I love You, Lord, and I yield my life and (name's) life to You. You are a God of miracles and mercy and the Lord of redemption and restoration.

Word of God

On My Lips

*Keep this Book of the Law always on your
lips; meditate on it day and night, so that you
may be careful to do everything written in
it. Then you will be prosperous and successful.*

JOSHUA 1:8

Lord, how I love Your Word! I have hidden Your Word in my heart so that I might not sin against You. In times of crisis, Your Word has been a healing balm on my soul. I never want to take Your Word for granted.

Please help me to invest more time reading and memorizing Scripture, to meditate on it day and night so I can clearly hear from You and receive direction, especially regarding the many decisions I must make concerning my adult child. Help me to rest in the wisdom and power of Your Word.

Thank You for the healing, hope, and happiness I feel when I'm communicating with You through prayer and learning from You through Your Word. Thank You, Lord, for this holy book of wisdom and truth. May Your Word always be on my lips.

Word of God

Your Word Helps Me Wait

My soul, wait silently for God alone,
For my expectation is from Him.
He only is my rock and my salvation;
He is my defense; I shall not be moved.

PSALM 62:5-6 NKJV

Father, I pray for strength today as I wait on You. Through Your Word and Your Spirit, please give me wisdom and direction as I wait for You to answer my prayers. I confess that Your thoughts are not my thoughts, and Your ways are not my ways. Even when I feel as if I've been waiting a long time, and even when the circumstances in my life (or in my adult child's life) look grim, I will wait on You before I take action so I can be sure I'm following Your will.

God, we need a miracle to heal the hurts in our family. Thank You for being a God of miracles. Show us how to cooperate with You. May love, acceptance, and forgiveness abound in our home as we look to You for help. My hope is in You, O Lord. I trust in You alone.

Word of God

Faith Comes by Hearing

Faith comes by hearing,
and hearing by the word of God.

ROMANS 10:17 NKJV

Lord, as I open the Word of God today, I'm reminded of the many saints who were men and women of great faith. You did incredible things in their lives and changed the world through them. Yet they were people just like me, just like my adult child. They faced hard times and had many struggles in life, just as we do. But in all their trials, they continued to believe. Their faith brought them victory.

Father, strengthen my faith and my daughter's (son's) faith. Your Word tells us that faith comes by hearing and hearing by the Word of God. Lord, please increase my faith today so that Your life might flow through me. Lord, I want to have a pure heart and teachable spirit. Please give me supernatural wisdom and discernment, and guide my every thought and every decision.

Thank You Lord, for You are faithful. I praise Your holy name.

Word of God

Held Captive

*The word of God is alive and powerful. It is sharper
than the sharpest two-edged sword, cutting between
soul and spirit, between joint and marrow. It
exposes our innermost thoughts and desires.*

HEBREWS 4:12 NLT

Lord, I love Martin Luther's declaration that his conscience was held captive by the Word of God. How I long for my adult child to be in that kind of "bondage" rather than the bondage of addiction. Help (name) to understand that Your Word is living, that when we love Your Word, it lives in us and changes us from the inside out.

Father, please help my adult child discover the power of Your Word. Help (name) filter out the noise of the world and listen to the still, small voice of Your Spirit. Help (name) to see that we must receive the entire Word of God as teaching for our own good, even when it doesn't feel good.

God, in the changing currents of this world, may Your Word become the anchor of wisdom that keeps (name) from going adrift. When the wind and waves would overwhelm her (him), may Your Word carry her (him) safely to You.

The Captain of All Ships

You must worship only the LORD your God.
He is the one who will rescue you
from all your enemies.

2 KINGS 17:39 NLT

Lord, my pastor once talked about four important ships that sail on the sea of life—fellow*ship*, relation-*ship*, disciple*ship*, and lord*ship*. He said we must travel on all of these ships to grow closer to You. He also said the enemy is always trying to get us to abandon ship.

Father, I pray that You will plant (name) in a community of believers who will surround her (him) with loving, encouraging fellowship. May she (he) develop an ever-deepening relationship with You. May she (he) find leaders who will guide her (him) through wise and caring discipleship. And may she (he) come to depend on Your lordship as the guiding light by which she (he) navigates throughout life.

Please show (name) how to trust and love You as her (his) Captain on this journey of life, and remove the threat of any enemy that would try to lead her (him) astray.

A Worshipful Heart

Come, let us bow down in worship,
let us kneel before the LORD our Maker.

PSALM 95:6

Glorious Lord, You alone are worthy of praise and honor. Oh, how I long for my adult child to turn his (her) eyes upward and recognize You as King of kings and Lord of lords. You are the great healer and our keeper. Please give (name) a desire to worship and adore You.

Our worship glorifies You and transforms us. It gives us a more eternal viewpoint. Wonderful God, I praise You even in the midst of my pain. As Paul and Silas sang praises in prison, so I sing Your praises here and now—even before I see my adult child set free from the bondage of worldly lies. I praise You for always being with us. You are mighty to save and have saved me through Jesus Christ. You are perfect. You are love, and You love my children even more than I ever could. You are unchanging, and You never give up on us.

You are my hope, dear Lord. My eyes are on You, and I entrust my adult child to You.

Y—YIELD Everything to God

The "Y" Step in SANITY

The Spirit of the Sovereign LORD is upon me,
for the LORD has anointed me
to bring good news to the poor.
He has sent me to comfort the brokenhearted
and to proclaim that captives will be released
and prisoners will be freed.

ISAIAH 61:1 NLT

Heavenly Father, I come before You today with open hands and an open heart as I release my adult child to You. Lord, please help (name) change the attitudes and behaviors that he (she) needs to change. And help me remember that the only person I can change is me. As I yield my son (daughter) to You, help him (her) to yield himself (herself) to You as well. Show (name) the difference between surrendering to You and just giving up. Help him (her) to see the wisdom of entrusting himself (herself) to You, the infinitely powerful Caregiver.

Lord God, give me strength to step out of the way as You work in (name's) life. Thank You for helping me to jump off the gerbil wheel of insanity and release (name) to Your love, mercy, and grace.

Fix My Brokenness

The LORD rescues the godly;
he is their fortress in times of trouble.
PSALM 37:39 NLT

Lord, I long for joy but I am so full of sorrow. I am lost as to what I can do to help (name). He (she) chooses to do whatever brings instant gratification regardless of the consequences. He (she) is slowly slipping away, yet I'm the one who is at the breaking point. I come today to yield (name) to You. I know I can no longer get in the way, because every time I try to help, things only get worse.

Please fix my brokenness as I stop trying to fix my child. Show me what I need to do to reclaim the peace and joy I've lost over the years. Help me establish healthy boundaries and repair broken walls that will protect my heart without hardening it.

Father, You are my only hope, and I'm willing to do whatever it takes to return to sanity and get back the life I once knew, the life I know You want me to have. Thank You, Lord, for being my fortress.

Y—YIELD Everything to God
A Bold New Journey

Anyone who belongs to Christ has become a new person. The old life is gone; a new life has begun!
2 Corinthians 5:17 NLT

Heavenly Father, I'm ready to regain sanity and find peace in my life.

The time has come for me to respond differently to people with whom I've had weak and unhealthy boundaries—including my adult child. I'm ready to make a course correction. This won't be easy for me to implement, and it won't be easy for some people to accept. Please, Lord, give me the wisdom and the words to convey my changes to those I love in a way that is pleasing to You and respectful to them.

I need Your supernatural strength in this journey to get off the gerbil wheel of insanity.

Thank You, Lord, for bringing sanity into what was once a chaotic life. Take control and guide me on this path to hope and healing. I YIELD everything to You, and I embrace the new person I am in Christ. I praise Your holy name and will love, honor, and obey You all the days of my life.

SANITY Support Group Creed

To be read aloud every week by a Group Member volunteer.

(substitute him/her as needed)

I cannot change the life of my adult child, no matter how much I would like to. However, I can change myself and the choices I make. Today I will make choices based on love, not anger. I will set healthy boundaries with my adult child by choosing to follow the 6-Steps to SANITY. What my adult child does with his life is his choice. I will no longer accept responsibility for his choices. I will be firm and loving at the same time. I will stop thinking it is selfish to focus on my own health and well-being. I will love my adult child—and myself—enough to let go of my own negative habits. I understand pain is often necessary for God to do His best work, and I choose to let God do a good work in me—and in the life of my adult child.

I will gain SANITY and take back my life!

Bible Versions Used

Setting Boundaries®
with Your Adult Children

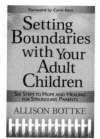

If you enjoyed Allison's *One-Minute Prayers for Your Adult Children,* you'll want to read her bestselling book *Setting Boundaries for Your Adult Children: Six Steps to Hope and Healing for Struggling Parents.*

This important and compassionate book will help parents and grandparents of the many adult children who continue to make life painful for their loved ones. Writing from firsthand experience, Allison identifies the lies that kept her and her son in bondage—and how she overcame them. Additional real-life stories from other parents are woven through the text.

A tough-love book to help readers cope with dysfunctional adult children, *Setting Boundaries with Your Adult Children* will empower families by offering hope and healing through SANITY—a six-step program to help parents regain control in their homes and in their lives.

Allison Bottke is the award-winning author of the acclaimed Setting Boundaries books (more than 150,000 sold), which includes *Setting Boundaries with Your Adult Children, Setting Boundaries with Your Aging Parents, Setting Boundaries with Difficult People, Setting Boundaries with Food, Setting Boundaries for Women,* and *The Young Women's Guide to Setting Boundaries.* She is the founder of the SANITY Support Group, an outreach based on the Setting Boundaries series. Her other books include the God Answers Prayers series, and she is the founder and general editor of more than a dozen volumes in the popular *God Allows U-Turns* anthology. She has written or edited more than 30 nonfiction and fiction books and is a frequent guest on national radio and TV programs. Allison lives in the Dallas/Fort Worth area.

Visit Allison's website at
SettingBoundariesBooks.com

To learn more about Harvest House books and
to read sample chapters, visit our website:

www.harvesthousepublishers.com

HARVEST HOUSE PUBLISHERS
EUGENE, OREGON